Shots Fired
Surviving an Active Shooter/Assailant

Joseph B. Walker

ARCHWAY
PUBLISHING

Archway Publishing books may be ordered through booksellers or by contacting:

Archway Publishing
1663 Liberty Drive
Bloomington, IN 47403
www.archwaypublishing.com
1 (888) 242-5904

ISBN: 978-1-4808-4622-7 (sc)
ISBN: 978-1-4808-4623-4 (e)

Library of Congress Control Number: 2017905603

Print information available on the last page.

Archway Publishing rev. date: 06/05/2017

Table of Contents

Introduction

....

As you are about to walk into your place of work, you hear several popping sounds. From cases occurring throughout the nation, you think it might be gunshots, but you quickly dismiss that thought from your mind. Workplace shootings happen elsewhere—not in your city and definitely not at your company! Just then, you hear people screaming and see them running toward you. Some of them have blood on their clothing. One of the people in the group says that there is a former employee with a gun who is shooting people. You start running to try and escape. As you round a corner, you inadvertently come face to face with the armed assailant ...

Or:

You have stopped at the local mall's food court for a quick bite to eat. Suddenly, a male begins attacking a female with a knife, stabbing her several times before severing her head. He then attacks another woman and starts to run in your direction. You have a license to carry a concealed weapon and have your weapon in your possession ...

In both cases, your initial thoughts are: *What should I do? Should I try to run? Should I raise my hands and try to convince him that I don't want to die? Should I try to intervene? Why aren't the police here right now to deal with this?* Well, read on, as I have crucial information needed to detect and defend against an active shooter before, during, and after shots have been fired, or against an assailant armed with an edged weapon.

The million-dollar question for politicians, organizational leaders, and those who either directly or indirectly provide for our safety is, "Has everything been done to protect innocent citizens against an active shooter/assailant?" I believe the answer is no! A behind-the-scenes examination has uncovered several reasons why enough has not been done. These reasons are alarming and wide-ranging.

Protection of their fiefdom, their ego, their ignorance to the threat and their own self-righteous arrogance is often the primary reason behind the inaction of people in key positions who could take significant actions to adequately address the threats. They have been lulled into complacency. Although they have a responsibility to safeguard our school children, private citizens, their business clients, and their countless employees, they fail to act. Some officials believe such shootings only happen elsewhere and will never occur at their location. Some flatly refuse to listen to strategies or implement training to mitigate such a threat. In fact, often their actions have only been those quick and easy steps required to say they have addressed the threat when, in reality, their lack of effort has continued to place everyone at risk.

Sanctuary from an active shooter/assailant in the public or private sectors does not exist. These events have occurred, and will occur, across an extremely broad spectrum in our society and have touched numerous communities. In the past, these events have transpired in, on, or around every type of school campus (from elementary schools through private and public colleges), places of worship, fast-food restaurants, and mass entertainment venues, as well as a variety of workplaces. With the sheer number of active shooting cases and the variety of methodologies used by each shooter/assailant, much more is required to save lives than the contemporary strategies currently in place and taught by any number of so-called leading authorities advocating minimal training in life-and-death situations.

During my employment with the Reno Police Department before I retired after twenty-five years of service, rising to the rank of lieutenant, and my almost ten years with United States Homeland Security, I was privy to a plethora of reports on threats against our civilian and military population. In my pursuit of excellence as a ninth-degree black belt in martial arts, I won numerous karate championship titles in several states. From all of my experience, I know that I can do more to help people stay safe than what is being offered by industry experts. Throughout forty-five years of diligent study in martial arts, and during both of my careers in public safety, my agenda has always been to help save innocent lives.

My dedicated years of training, as well as my various skills and abilities, have allowed me to construct a proactive and multifaceted approach that encompasses all of the relevant elements necessary for an affirmative defense against the active shooter/assailant. My approach enhances the current industry-embraced concepts taught by most law enforcement agencies using the terminology **Escape**, **Shelter to Hide**, and **Shelter to Fight** instead of just Run, Hide, and Fight. This paradigm shift provides details that are absent from the current industry concept in addition to the tactics and techniques necessary to implement this approach during an event.

This work is designed to provide information about the active shooter/assailant that will educate everyone from the novice, who may now only have a minimal amount of information on this threat, to the business manager, who has much more material on this subject, on a number of proactive and reactive measures needed to mitigate the threat of an active shooter/assailant. Addressing the threat also requires using observational skills to understand the pre-incident behaviors of the prospective subject. Preemptive facility strategies are provided as well. Also discussed are methods to **escape** the kill zone and details of how to **shelter and hide** for people who may be unable or unwilling to actively participate in fighting for their own lives.

Included in this book are personal defensive techniques that are specifically designed to physically engage and prevail against the active shooter/assailant. The defensive techniques are practical, easy, and effective physical movements designed to defeat an assailant armed with a knife, handgun, or long gun. All physical techniques emphasize economy of motion. That is, when an assailant launches an armed attack, each defensive technique disarms the assailant and allows the defender to use that weapon against an assailant who continues to pose a deadly threat. When the defender becomes proficient in these techniques, these defensive actions will become one quick, fluid, and continuous movement. The techniques are described in step-by-step instructions that are accompanied by photographs to illustrate how to physically engage and disarm the armed assailant. This work will also speak to the members of our society who are legally armed, providing them tactical information on how and when to successfully engage the active shooter/assailant, if forced into such a deadly encounter.

Included within this book is a collection of active shooter/assailant cases that will serve to corroborate specific points. All references to past victims are not meant to cast or assign blame, but are only used as teaching aids for illustration of the technical and tactical aspects of a successful defensive strategy, as well as to prevent others from making deadly tactical or technical errors. Law enforcement agencies use a similar strategy in their debriefing of critical incidents to improve the future performance of their personnel. Excluded are the names of the shooters/assailants, for there is no reason to give them any more press than has already been afforded to them for their cowardly acts of pandemonium and needless carnage.

Who Should Read This Book

I found the instruction booklet for a printer to provide greater detail than any training I have seen afforded to the general public on how to survive or defeat an active shooter/assailant. It is for that reason that I provide specific and detailed information on how to address this threat. The suggested audience for this book is anyone truly concerned about how to effectively reduce the threat, death toll, and casualty rates of an active shooter/assailant. This book is also for the employees in any work environment (private and public sector), from the CEO to the custodian and everyone in between, who want to know exactly what to do in a deadly workplace attack, rather than be forced to make those important decisions "on the fly" with limited information. This book is also for the countless citizens who go on vacations to other states or countries where it is forbidden to have either a concealed weapon or any firearm. And lastly, this book is for the average person who is continuously bombarded with incidents of active shootings but has never been afforded the venue to receive any instruction in this subject. For the person who desires to learn how to avoid or safely escape a violent altercation and what to do if forced to fight for their life.

This book is intended to provide the reader with a more in-depth and insightful knowledge of the active shooter/assailant, as well as to illustrate some common sense tools, tactics, and techniques to give the defender a fighting chance at surviving an armed encounter against such an assailant. It is my intent that any and all information, tactics, and physical techniques included within this work will be 100 percent successful. However, just as in life, there are no guarantees. Anything can happen, as there are many variables to contend with. I believe the alternative to fighting back is to do nothing and hope either that someone else comes to your aid in time to rescue you before the shooter/assailant has taken either your life or the lives of those you hold dear, or that the deadly attacker will stop before getting to you or your loved ones. I would never advocate for any person to leave 100 percent of their safety in the hands of others who have not taken every safeguard to effectively mitigate the threat, or who have not even considered doing so. In a time where authorities are either busy contemplating what to do or flatly refusing to believe such a threat can occur, we have to be responsible for our own safety.

You should be prepared mentally, physically, and spiritually to take action should that fateful time ever arise. You should be capable of using your own power to educate yourself and to arm yourself with information, tactics, and techniques to defeat the active shooter/assailant.

Part 1
Understanding the Threat

The Shooters/Assailants

Definition of an Active Shooter/Assailant

The active shooter/assailant is a person who, while using a firearm or any other deadly weapon, is actively killing or attempting to kill people in a public or private place. The assailant can be of any age, gender, sexual orientation, race, or ethnic identification. The shooter/assailant needs only to be capable of obtaining (legally or otherwise) a deadly weapon and using that weapon against people. Active shooters/assailants have used a multitude of weapons, including handguns, long guns, rifles, shotguns, knives and improvised explosive devices (IEDs) to commit their crimes.

Past shooters and assailants have come from a broad spectrum in our society. We have seen elementary school children from Jonesboro, Arkansas; middle school children from Sparks, Nevada; teenagers from Columbine High School in Colorado; college students from Virginia Tech; and adults through their late eighties. Overall, their ages range from children to elderly adults and comprise nearly every race, ethnicity, and gender. Their occupations include students, educators, blue- and white-collar workers, retired professionals, and military personnel.

Internally based threats are comprised of people who naturally belong to a particular environment. For school shootings, these shooters would be current or former students, educators, or school employees. For a business, they would include current or former employees of that business. These assailants have intricate and detailed knowledge of the environment and potentially a contingency/evacuation plan. Their knowledge of the facility and the location of their intended targets make them a cause of extra concern. The ease with which these assailants can covertly bring their weapons into the killing zone is higher due to their non-suspicious appearance and/or their ability to bring in items, typically without suspicion, on a daily basis.

Externally based threats are those who may or may not regularly visit or belong to that particular environment and usually will not have intricate knowledge of the facility's emergency or evacuation plans. Examples of this type of assailant could be the spouse, significant other, or relative of a person who may, or may not, have any legitimate business at that location. Another example could also be a dissatisfied customer of the business.

The *other threats* comprise those who don't easily fall into the internally or externally based threats groupings. These assailants are those who have no apparent tie to any of the victims or to the shooting location. Examples of this type of assailant could be criminals who are actively engaged in gunfire with law enforcement officers during the commission of a violent crime, or in an effort to escape. They could also be mentally deranged individuals who want to kill randomly or terrorists who have chosen that targeted location for currently unknown motives.

American Active Shooters

One of the first widely publicized active shooting cases in America was at the University of Texas Tower in Austin, Texas, on August 1, 1966. The shooter, a former marine, chose that day to ascend to the top of the University of Texas Bell Tower observation deck with a variety of weapons. The firepower brought with him consisted of the following: an M-1 carbine rifle, a 12-gauge semi-automatic shotgun, a Remington hunting rifle, a .35 caliber pump rifle, a .30 caliber carbine, a 9 mm Luger pistol, a .25 caliber pistol, a .357 Magnum revolver, hundreds of rounds of ammunition, a machete, and three knives. He also brought other supplies, such as food, coffee, vitamins, medication, earplugs, water, matches, lighter fluid, rope, binoculars, a transistor radio, toilet paper, a razor for shaving, and deodorant.

The shooting began at 11:48 a.m. and continued until 1:24 p.m., when the shooter was shot dead by police who ultimately ascended onto the observation deck to stop the shooter. The shooting took the lives of fifteen people and wounded another thirty-two people. The youngest of the shooting victims was sixteen, and the oldest was fifty-eight. Among the deceased were women, men, and one teenager. Law enforcement learned from this event and formed Special Weapons and Tactics (SWAT) teams to address subsequent problems of this type.

"Going postal" became a term assigned to disgruntled United States postal workers who used firearms to settle their grievances. On August 19, 1983, a resigned postal employee entered the post office in Johnston, South Carolina, with a 12-gauge shotgun and shot at workers in the hallway. The shooter killed the postmaster and wounded two other employees. From August 19, 1983, to the present day, forty-seven people have lost their lives and another twenty-three people have been injured in active shootings at postal institutions throughout the United States.

Another mass shooting occurred inside a McDonald's in San Ysidro, California. On July 18, 1984, the shooter entered the restaurant and fatally shot twenty-one people and injured nineteen others. The shooter carried a 9 mm Uzi semi-automatic, a 12-guage shotgun, and a 9 mm pistol. The shooting lasted for seventy-seven minutes before the assailant was fatally shot by a SWAT team sniper. The shooter fired 257 rounds at his victims, who were predominantly Mexican and

Mexican-American and ranged in age from eight months to seventy-four years of age.

On April 16, 2007, at 9:45 a.m., on the college campus of Virginia Tech, a total of thirty-three students and faculty were killed by a gunman who had chained and locked the doors of a campus building from the inside prior to his shooting spree. Whether the doors were chained to keep his potential victims inside or the police from entering the area until he completed his shootings will never be known, as the shooter took his own life before that and numerous other questions could be answered.

On July 20, 2012, at a movie theater in Aurora, Colorado, at the premier showing of the newest Batman movie, the shooter left the theater and re-entered dressed in bulletproof clothing, a gas mask, and a Kevlar helmet. The shooter ignited a gas grenade and began shooting the patrons inside the dark theater. After killing twelve people and wounding fifty-eight others, the shooter left the theater and surrendered outside to police.

On May 23, 2014, a college student at the University of California, Santa Barbara, began his killing spree by killing three of his roommates. He then killed three other people and wounded thirteen others before he committed suicide. The killer provided his rationale for the murders via a social media post, stating a desire to punish women for rejecting him and a desire to punish sexually active men for living a better life than his.

On December 5, 2014, a man using a knife stabbed four people during their train ride from Chicago, Illinois, to Huron, Michigan. The police were alerted to a suspicious person. When police arrived, the suspect was in the process of randomly stabbing people. Police were able to use a Taser to stop the attack. The reason for the attack is unknown.

The active shooter/assailant's tactics appears to evolve with each event that occurs. It appears that potential shooters observe what others before them have done and sometimes alter one or two factors for their particular deadly event. Whether they want higher body counts or greater notoriety than their predecessors, the result is the same: innocent lives are needlessly lost.

Foreign Active Shooters

On November 17, 1997, six armed gunman massacred sixty-two people at a tourist attraction at the Temple of Hatshepsut in Egypt. The gunmen, armed with automatic weapons and knives, disguised themselves as members of the security forces. They killed two armed guards and, with the tourists trapped inside the temple, the killing went on for forty-five minutes. The killers used both guns and butcher knives. Four Egyptians were killed, including three police officers and a tour guide, along with fifty-eight foreign tourists. The six gunmen were also killed.

On October 23, 2002, at a Russian movie theater, armed terrorists took 850 hostages. After a two-and-a-half-day siege, Russian forces pumped chemical agents into the building's ventilation system before they entered the theater. During the raid, forty attackers were killed by Russian forces; however, 130 hostages died due to adverse reactions to the chemical agent used to subdue the shooters.

Beginning on September 1, 2004, the Beslan School siege in Russia lasted three days and involved the capture of over 1,100 people as hostages (including 777 children). A group of armed militants occupied the school and, on the third day of the crisis, Russian security forces entered the building with tanks, rockets, and other heavy weapons. At least 334 hostages were killed, including 186 children.

In Oslo, Norway, on July 22, 2011, a male suspect, dressed in a uniform from the Oslo Police Department, boarded a ferry to the island of Utoya, where a youth camp which was held every summer. This particular year, there were approximately 600 teenagers attending the camp. The lone suspect presented himself as a police officer to camp officials and then killed two of them. The suspect then asked people to gather around him. The suspect produced his weapons and began indiscriminately firing, killing and wounding numerous people. He first shot people on the island and later starting shooting at people who were trying to escape by swimming across the lake. In just over an hour, the gunman killed seventy-seven people. Once police ultimately arrived on the island, the gunman surrendered. The suspect claimed to have been planning for the shooting since 2002 (nine years earlier) and preparing for the attack since 2009, even though he was able to conceal his violent intentions from others. The suspect visited firing ranges to sharpen his skills, and according to his manifesto, he made use of video games as a training aid as well as to hone his shooting skills using an in-game holographic sight similar to the one he used during the attacks.

On February 3, 2014, an upperclassman of a school in northern Moscow, Russia, shot and killed a teacher and a police officer. The attacker entered the school armed with a rifle, shot a police officer, and then opened fire on others who arrived at the scene. The student held more than twenty other students hostage before he was disarmed and taken into custody. The student hostages were all freed.

At a beach on a resort in Sousse, Tunisia, a gunman began shooting randomly, killing thirty-eight people and injuring at least thirty-nine others. The Islamic State claimed responsibility for the attack. Among the casualties were citizens from Britain, Belgium, France, Germany, and Ireland. One wounded man ran into the sea to escape the carnage.

On November 13, 2015, six different attacks occurred at various sites throughout Paris, France, in which at least eight members of the Islamic State used bullets and suicide belts, ultimately killing 130 people. The shootings and killings involved patrons at restaurants, a concert venue, and a soccer game. Surveillance footage that was released and appeared on the news illustrated how one of the shooters approached a scene that had been sprayed with bullets from a semi-automatic rifle. The shooter walked within two feet of a woman who was sheltering underneath a table outside the restaurant. The shooter pointed his rifle at the woman's head and pulled the trigger three times, only for the weapon to fail to discharge each time. The shooter then walked away from the woman, who ultimately ran into the restaurant for shelter.

Copycats

On August 10, 2012, police arrested a twenty-nine-year-old in Ostrava, in the Czech Republic. The police had information that the suspect was preparing a copycat shooting inspired by the 2011 Oslo attacks in Norway. The suspect was stockpiling weapons (including a full-automatic assault rifle and armor-piercing bullets) and had converted an aerial bomb for remote detonation. The suspect had the remote control with him while arrested. He had also obtained uniforms of the Czech police and of the Czech prison service, as well as a police ID. The suspect had four prior criminal convictions, including a six-month-long suspended sentence for setting off an explosive that demolished an empty wooden cottage. On April 3, 2013, a court in Ostrava found the suspect criminally insane. He was also found dangerous to the public and ordered into psychiatric detention. The reasons for detention shall be reviewed by the court periodically every two years.

On November 20, 2012, Polish authorities arrested a forty-five-year-old lecturer at the Agricultural University of Cracow under suspicion of preparing a similar attack. The suspect was an admirer of the suspect in the Oslo shooting and was further inspired by the Oklahoma City Federal Building bombing. The Polish domestic intelligence service first found out about the suspect after it launched investigation into the suspect's Polish contacts, when it became known that he had ordered some of the chemicals for his bomb from Poland online. The suspect wanted to detonate explosives in a car parked outside the parliament building in Warsaw, Poland. The suspect reportedly stated that the suspects in Oslo and in the Oklahoma City bombing had made mistakes, but that he would be better.

On March 27, 2008, police in Homestead, Florida, arrested a

twenty-year-old Asian American individual for making threats online. The subject made statements that he would cause the next Virginia Tech. Several pistols, four AK-47s, and a .50 BMG were seized from his house. The subject also possessed more than 6000 rounds of ammunition.

On June 17, 2014, a University of Washington student was arrested after he praised the killings in Santa Barbara, California, via social media and stated that he would kill women. This would-be copycat wrote that everything the Santa Barbara killer did was perfectly justified and that he was the next killer of this type. This student stated, "Guess what, I'll do the right thing this time. I'll make sure I only kill women" (mynorthwest.com 17/0614). There were reports that the University of Washington newspaper received threatening phone calls and sororities found chalk outlines (similar to those you'd find at a murder scene) outside their houses. The suspect was arrested for cyberstalking and felony harassment.

Suffice it to say that killers and potential killers do look at each other's work and, for their own warped and twisted reasons, strive to emulate that work. Some killers even state they will improve upon what has been done before them. In any event, we can only regretfully look forward to additional carnage to be perpetrated by one or more of these sick and twisted individuals.

Motivations for Violent Encounters

Domestic violence is prevalent in today's society and is not limited by race, gender, social status, or occupation. Domestic disputes can turn deadly with tragic results for either of the domestic partners or the responding officers. Sometimes, a domestic partner may not inflict deadly violence until a later time and place. On September 20, 2015, in Selma, Alabama, a man shot the mother of his child, his child, and a church official. The man was taken into custody and charged with three counts of attempted murder.

Stalking and domestic violence are directly correlated with shooting incidents. Stalking is typically defined as an activity where one person harasses, threatens, and frightens another person. The stalker often disregards legal and physical boundaries established by law and will act in a bizarre manner to harass, threaten, frighten, or inflict personal harm upon their victim. Stalkers are not restricted by gender, race, social economic status, or occupation. Stalking a person at work, school, home, church, or any other public or private place creates the potential for violent acts. Stalking is made even easier through access to the Internet and public records. If a person is determined to stalk another individual, there is no absolute guaranteed method to prevent that from happening. The criminal justice system can be employed to curtail or punish a stalker, but usually only after the stalker's reign of terror has already begun.

There are several categories that comprise the crime of stalking. *Simple obsessional* (the most common category) is a stalking category where the stalker and the victim either have had or are involved in a relationship. The behavior of the stalker toward the victim can be, but is not limited to, following the victim, destroying property, giving gifts, hurting the victim's pet, phone calls, text messages, letter writing, social media contacts, spreading lies or rumors, or physically hurting the victim.

An example of this type of stalking and shooting occurred in Seal Beach, California, on October 10, 2011. The male shooter, who was angry over his child custody case, entered a beauty salon where his estranged wife was employed. The shooter, dressed in body armor and armed with an AK-47 assault rifle, killed eight people, including his ex-wife. The shooter left the scene and later surrendered to police. When he was taken into custody, he advised police that he had even more guns in his truck.

The *love obsessional* type of stalker is a person who has never had a relationship with the victim. This type of stalker is a person who has somehow seen the victim and feels that there should be or is a relationship with the victim. The stalker will do whatever they can to establish and keep that relationship. The behavior can be the similar to that of the simple obsessional stalker.

One example of this type of stalking and subsequent shooting occurred at a company in Sunnyvale, California, on February 16, 1986. A female employee was being stalked by her male coworker, who wanted to have a relationship with her. After the stalker made numerous unwanted advances and attempts to establish a relationship, the worksite disciplined him, and a temporary restraining order (TPO) was obtained. A significant time after being served with the TPO and disciplined at that worksite, the male stalker came to the work armed with several guns and shot the target of his love obsession and several other coworkers. Luckily, the initial target survived, but seven other people were killed and four others were wounded.

Another type of stalking that can progress to a shooting incident involves the *revenge obsessional* stalker. This person is seeking revenge for some real or perceived act that was committed against them, their family, or others. This category of stalker will hold the offending party responsible for days, weeks, months, or even years. This stalker will plan the day, time, location, and act of vengeance they wants to inflict on the supposedly offending party or parties.

On December 17, 2013, at Urology of Nevada in Reno, Nevada, the shooter, who in 2010 had had a surgery from Urology of Nevada, claimed he was having adverse symptoms due to the surgery and returned to the facility. The fifty-one-year-old male entered the building carrying a shotgun and went to the third floor office area, where he ultimately shot and killed one doctor and wounded another doctor and a patron of the practice before taking his own life. The suspect was found to have three guns with him during the shooting: a 12-gauge shotgun, a .40 caliber handgun, and a derringer pistol. The suspect left notes at his home indicating his intent to commit the shootings and to subsequently commit suicide.

Another incident took place on December 14, 2010. The shooter entered an ongoing Panama City, Florida, school board meeting. Enraged over the firing of his wife, who had been employed by the school district, the shooter targeted the school board and allowed all others who were present to leave. After his rant, in which he announced that someone there was going to die that day, he opened fire on the school board. A security officer exchanged gunfire with the shooter, after which the shooter took his own life.

Another incident occurred in February 12, 2010, when a female college professor went on a shooting rampage during a faculty meeting at the University of Alabama in Huntsville. The shooter produced a 9 mm handgun and started shooting at each person in execution style, starting with the person closest to her. The shooter killed three colleagues and wounded three others. The reason given for the shooting was because she was angry over being denied tenure, which effectively ended her career.

Anger is a subcategory of motivation for the revenge obsessional stalker. In an anger-based attack, the assailant may or may not have any prior relationship with the victim or even know the victim but, based on their anger, the shooter will seek out persons and release that anger violently. The anger could be based on any number of things, including but not limited to the loss of a relationship or a job. The victims typically do not have any knowledge of the shooter's anger fixation.

On December 5, 2007, a shooter targeted people inside a shopping mall in Omaha, Nebraska, killing eight people and wounding five others. It was reported that the shooter was angry about losing his job and a breakup with his girlfriend prior to the shooting.

Another example of this type of category is from November 1, 2013, when a male entered Terminal Three of the Los Angeles International Airport and ultimately approached the Transportation Security Administration's security checkpoint. The subject produced an assault rifle, whereupon he shot and killed one TSA security officer and wounded three other people. The shooter then walked past the security checkpoint into the secure area and down the airport concourse. Airport police tracked and engaged the shooter near the terminal airline gates and food court, where the shooter was ultimately shot and taken into custody. According to several witnesses, the shooter approached them, asked if they were TSA agents, and then moved on when the witnesses said no. It was later determined that the suspect had a note in his possession that stated he wanted to kill TSA agents and described them as pigs.

Fame is a documented reason behind some shooting incidents. Some shooters and potential shooters have made it known that they desired to make a name for themselves and gain the fame that they had always (or at least recently) desired. Some desire to have their names added to the psychopaths' hall of fame, others want to go out in a blaze of glory and hail of bullets, while some explicitly want to obtain a higher body count than previous shooting events. After the Columbine High shooting of April 20, 1999, other school shooters have made reference to Columbine and stated that their desire was to obtain a higher body count or to be associated with these types of massacres.

Another example of the fame-seeking shooter is the 1981 attempted assassination of President Ronald Reagan. On March 30, President Ronald Reagan was leaving a speaking engagement in Washington, DC, when a gunman began shooting him from less than fifteen feet away. President Reagan was hit by a bullet that ricocheted off his vehicle. Although nobody was killed in the attack, Press Secretary James Brady was left paralyzed and permanently disabled. The suspect admitted the shooting was because he wanted to attract the attention of Hollywood actress Jodie Foster. Even though this was an assassination attempt on a president, the gunman fit the definition of an active shooter because he opened fire in an attempt to kill people in a public place.

Mental illness is a controversial element in discussion of shooting incidents. One might argue that every mass shooter/assailant is mentally ill. Any person wanting to kill innocent people whom they don't personally know and have no apparent connection to must be mentally ill.

There are cases that illustrate that mental illness is a factor in some active shooting events. In Carson City, Nevada, on September 6, 2011, at 8:58 a.m., a gunman arrived at a local restaurant in his minivan, got out, and shot a man on a motorcycle. The shooter then entered the restaurant carrying an assault rifle and shot several uniformed members of the Nevada National Guard. The guardsmen were all seated together having breakfast. Of the five guardsmen who were shot, three were fatally wounded. The shooter then shot other patrons inside the restaurant, killing a seventy-six-year-old woman. The shooter exited the restaurant and ultimately killed himself. The family of the shooter knew of his long history of mental illness and that he had access to numerous firearms.

Another case occurred on January 25, 2014, when a nineteen-year-old male stood in a dressing room at a store inside the mall of Columbia, Maryland, and took a photograph of himself holding a Mossberg 12-gauge shotgun. He uploaded the image to his social media blog, adding a note: "I had to do this. Today is the day. On previous days, I tried this and woke up with anxiety, regret, and hope for a better future. This day I didn't. I woke up [and] felt no emotions, no empathy, no sympathy. I will have freedom, or maybe not. I could care less" (Washington Times, 12/03/14). A moment later, the shooter stepped out of that store's dressing room and randomly killed two of the store's clerks before firing on other mall patrons. He wounded one shopper and sent hundreds of panicked shoppers and merchants racing for cover. Then he took his own life. The suspect had spent months searching the Internet for information about mass murder, focusing on the massacre at Columbine. He learned how to assemble and fire a shotgun and how to build a bomb. At the same time, the suspect sought out information on mental illness and joined a chatroom filled with people contemplating suicide. The police chief later said the suspect was dressed similarly to one of the Columbine gunmen, used a similar weapon, and lingered in the mall for forty-one minutes in order to time his attack to coincide with when the two students at Columbine High School began their killing rampage.

On July 23, 2015, a fifty-nine-year-old mentally ill man stood up inside a movie theater in Lafayette, Louisiana, and shot the two women seated in front of him. The shooter continued shooting at people, specifically seeking out women as his victims. Once police arrived, the suspect attempted to leave the theater but, for whatever reason, chose to return inside and ultimately took his own life. The suspect had a history of mental illness, and various disguises were located inside the suspect's vehicle and motel room.

And on January 6, 2017, a 26 year old Iraqi war veteran with a history of mental illness since his deployment, shot eleven people at the Ft. Lauderdale, Florida airport baggage claim area. According the various news reports, the shooter's family and significant other all concurred that the shooter was suffering from mental illness. In November of 2016, the shooter himself went to his local office of the F. B.I. in Anchorage, Alaska and made statements that he was being made to watch Islamic State terrorist propaganda videos. The yet to be shooter was relinquished to local law enforcement for a mental health evaluation.

Suicide by cop refers to a situation where a person is suicidal and has been, for whatever reason, unable to commit suicide. They will therefore take steps to engage law enforcement in an armed confrontation. This shooter may point, aim, or shoot at police officers, knowing that law enforcement officers will use deadly force to protect themselves. Hence, these shooters are both homicidal and suicidal. On January 23, 2011, a man walked into the Sixth Precinct in Detroit, Michigan, and opened fire with a pistol-grip shotgun. The man was able to shoot four police officers before other officers returned fire, killing the shooter.

Being bullied has been reported as the motivating factor behind several school shootings. Past school shooters have stated their motive for opening fire in their respective schools was being bullied by their peers at their schools. Although school officials have launched anti-bullying campaigns, some of these campaigns were in effect at the time of a particular school's shooting and do not appear to have helped prevent such incidents. Teachers must be vigilant in order to spot those skirmishes that are usually done out of the view of adults. Although children are expected to report when they are bullied, some children may be reluctant to do so. Parents need to be connected to their children and should educate them on all forms of bullying, whether it's person to person or cyberbullying via social media. Parents and school officials need to address these issues before they occur. Once a child is reported or discovered bullying another child, the bullying child needs to be held accountable for their behavior. This needs to be done throughout the child's educational experience. Also, the parents (of the bully), school officials, and law enforcement need to form a partnership in order to adequately address all the relevant issues before things get out of hand. It is highly unlikely that, if left unaddressed, a child bully will outgrow their behavior, and this will typically continue during their adult life.

Psychological bullying can be done by one or more people, either in person, online, on social media, or using any other written means to degrade that person verbally. The teasing could be to ridicule the person's sexuality, physique, intelligence, or any other imposed fault meant to cause that person embarrassment.

Physical bullying usually takes place in the form of physical violence that is meant to embarrass the person or break down their will. Although it can cause significant physical harm, it is typically meant to cause emotional and psychological harm to the victim.

On October 21, 2013, Sparks Middle School in Sparks, Nevada, was the site of a fatal shooting when a seventh-grade student entered the rear of the school playground area just prior to the start of school. The shooter shot two of his fellow students, who had reportedly bullied the shooter prior to that day. When a male teacher confronted the shooter, the teacher was shot and killed. The shooter then turned the gun on himself, taking his own life.

Workplace discipline is also an issue that can lead to violent attacks by the self-perceived victim. Inside the office of US Immigration and Customs Enforcement (ICE) in Los Angeles, California, a meeting on February 17, 2012, between a supervising agent and his subordinate led to a dispute over a discipline issue. It resulted in a shooting in which the subordinate agent fired several rounds at his supervisor, wounding him. An armed colleague intervened and fired at the shooter, killing him.

In Reno, Nevada, on October 29, 2010, an employee of Wal-Mart entered the store about 8:30 a.m. and started shooting in the direction of employees with a small caliber firearm. The forty-five-year-old suspect shot three Wal-Mart employees, one of whom was the manager. The shooter then barricaded himself inside the store until he ultimately surrendered to police. The shooter had been summoned to the store that morning to discuss impending disciplinary action.

Criminal activity often results in shooting incidents, either through police confrontation of a crime in progress or through confrontations between criminal organizations, such as gangs.

On September 19, 2013, an outdoor basketball game in Chicago, Illinois, erupted in gunfire, and thirteen people were shot and injured, including a three-year-old child. An assault-style rifle with a high-capacity magazine was used in the shooting, which appeared to be gang-related as reported by the Chicago Police superintendent.

In Sacramento, California, at a Good Guys electronic store, on April 1, 1991, four criminals entered the store to commit an armed robbery. The robbery was botched, and the criminals took hostages of the fifty customers and employees who remained inside the store. Police attempted to negotiate with the hostage-takers, but the situation deteriorated when a SWAT sniper missed his target. One of the criminals began shooting the hostages. The SWAT team exited their concealed position in the back of the store and stormed the hostage-takers. Three of the hostages were killed by the criminals, and three of the four hostage-takers were killed as well. The fourth hostage-taker was captured and prosecuted.

Hate crimes are also responsible for shooting incidents across the US. On June 17, 2014, a twenty-one-year-old white male purposely sought out a historic African American church in Charleston, South Carolina, and entered the church during their Bible study. Because the regular participants of the church included the new person into their Bible study, he stated that he was almost convinced not to go through with his original plan—which was to shoot and kill several of the members.

The shooter ultimately produced a handgun and began shooting, killing nine people. The shooter used racial slurs while he reloaded his weapon several times and continued his murderous rampage. The shooter intentionally left one of the parishioners alive so she could relate the carnage. After killing his victims, the suspect fled the scene in a vehicle and was captured the following day in Shelby, North Carolina, by law enforcement. The shooter had posted a picture on social media that showed him with the Confederate flag and wearing a jacket with two flag patches from Rhodesia (during their apartheid era), which are popular with white supremacists.

Domestic terrorism is when an act of terror is committed on American soil and is perpetrated by a person that appears to be an American citizen. These individuals plot against America from within its borders and will stop at nothing to cause mass destruction, even if it kills their friends or neighbors. These people are usually well-concealed within the fabric of our society, and they do not bring attention to themselves by their activities. They may work in a variety of jobs or participate in activities within a community while simultaneously plotting how they can carry out their act of terror. The domestic terrorist has an ideology that is motivated toward violence.

In recent cases, the terrorists use a variety of means to commit their act(s) of terror. These people look just like you and me and are usually not acting or dressing in ways that bring attention to themselves.

And in some cases, individuals do bring attention to themselves, but authorities either fail to connect the dots or refuse to even admit the dots are even present.

On November 5, 2009, at 1:34 p.m., a US Army major, a psychiatrist, entered the Soldier Readiness Processing Center at Fort Hood. Armed with an FN 57 pistol with two laser sights, he fatally shot thirteen people and injured more than thirty others. According to eyewitnesses, the shooter bowed his head for several seconds, suddenly stood up and shouted *"Allahu Akbar,"* and then started shooting. Days after the shooting, reports in the media revealed that a joint terrorism task force had been aware of e-mail communications between the shooter and the Yemen-based Imam Anwar al-Awlaki, who had been monitored by the National Security Agency as a security threat. It was also learned that the shooter's colleagues had been aware of his increasing Islamic radicalization for several years. Although the incident was listed as "workplace violence," numerous sources disagree and categorize the shooting as a terrorist act.

On June 8, 2014, a husband and wife team (aged thirty-one and twenty-two respectively) walked into a pizza restaurant in Las Vegas, Nevada, and approached two Las Vegas police officers on their lunch break. According to one witness, who was seated behind the officers, the male walked up to the officers, yelled out that this was a revolution, and shot one of the officers in the head. The other officer was then shot in the throat. Both suspects fired multiple rounds into one officer's body. The male shooter took one of the officers' handguns. One of the two shooters covered the officers' bodies with a yellow flag that contained an image of a coiled snake and the words "Don't tread on me" and then placed a swastika on his body. The suspects left the restaurant, entered a nearby Wal-Mart department store, and fired a shot into the air. A customer inside the store, who was legally armed and unaware of the couple's earlier murders, confronted the male suspect who had fired the shot. Not realizing the male was accompanied by his female accomplice, he was shot and killed. As other customers fled the store, the armed couple went toward the rear of the store. Police soon arrived and entered the store, where they confronted the armed couple. Although the suspects exchanged gunfire with police, the male suspect was fatally shot, and the female suspect took her own life. Law enforcement investigators later discovered paraphernalia associated with white supremacism, including swastika symbols, and literature expressing the ideology that law enforcement was the oppressor.

Domestic terrorism can be motivated in a variety of ways. Inmates from any US prison can become radicalized and convert to a form of Islam. Authorities call this form of radicalization "Prislam," as it a violent interpretation of Islam that is disconnected from the majority of modern practice. Those who convert are former gang members and other convicted felons that have already demonstrated a hostile and violent lifestyle. They are looking for a method to express their hostility and a group who will sanction violent acts.

Other domestic terrorists have been members of our US military. This was brought to light after a double homicide was discovered on December 5, 2011, near the Fort Stewart army base, southwest of Savannah, Georgia. The victims were a former army private and his seventeen-year-old girlfriend. On December 10, authorities arrested four active-duty army personnel. The killing was intended to silence the victims so they could not expose the activities of the domestic terror group of which the male victim had been a member. The group was a paramilitary militia organization who wanted to overthrow the US government and assassinate the president. The group wanted to poison food supplies, blow up a hydroelectric dam, and create a nuclear catastrophe. The group had acquired a multitude of assault weapons and spent $87,000 on bomb components and other weapons.

During the summer of 2014, a terrorist organization calling themselves the Islamic State emerged in the Middle East. The group has committed a host of repulsive acts, including the beheading of two American citizens. On September 26, 2014, in Moore, Oklahoma, a woman was beheaded at a food distribution center by a coworker.

The thirty-year-old male suspect had recently been suspended from work and had returned to exact revenge. The suspect reportedly had converted to Islam and had attempted to also convert others at work to Islam. The suspect drove to the front of the business and struck a vehicle before he walked inside. He then attacked the fifty-four-year-old female employee using a knife, stabbing her several times before severing her head. He then stabbed another woman. When other employees attempted to intervene, the suspect chased them away with his knife. The company's CEO, who was a reserve county sheriff's deputy, shot the suspect as he continued his attack on the second woman. The suspect survived and was transported to the hospital. Whether this was the effort of a terrorist lone wolf from some Islamic group bringing domestic terror to the United States or just another attack and killing that occurred in the workplace, the results are the same: the loss of yet another life.

On October 23, 2014 in Queens, New York, one man attacked four police officers with a hatchet. Although the suspect was able to strike two of the four police officers with his hatchet, the other officers were able to shoot and mortally wound the suspect. One of the officers was hospitalized with a head wound. The suspect's image was caught on surveillance camera as he ran toward the officers and, using both hands, raised his hatchet just moments before the attack. The New York police commissioner called this a terrorist attack by a homegrown radical. The suspect was a Muslim convert who ranted online against America and had used his computer to browse for organized terror groups and beheadings.

In Chattanooga, Tennessee, on July 16, 2015, one gunman purposefully sought out members of the United States military in two different locations in order to shoot them. The first location was a military recruiting center, where the gunman fired shots from his vehicle into the glass front of the building. The suspect, armed with an assault rifle, two other long guns and one handgun, then drove his vehicle to the Naval Operations Support Center, a separate military site, where he engaged and killed five service personnel. Police were able to locate the gunman at that second location and shot and killed the suspect. The FBI considered the suspect a homegrown violent extremist who perpetrated this act of violence on his own. It was later learned that the shooter, born in Kuwait, had immigrated to the United States in the late 1990s with his parents. The parents were reported to have practiced and maintained a conservative and strict Muslim lifestyle. The suspect was reported to have sought treatment for depression and bipolar disorder.

Orlando, Florida, was the site of what was called one of the worst mass shootings in the United States since the attack of September 11, 2001. A lone gunman armed with two firearms entered a nightclub frequented by the queer community and opened fire, killing forty-nine and injuring at least fifty others. During the attack, the gunman himself telephoned 911 and claimed he was inspired by ISIS. The gunman took the time to use social media as well as communicate with his wife. Police ultimately arrived and engaged the shooter, who fled to the nightclub's bathroom, where he took a number of hostages. After at least a three-hour standoff, the police were able to break through a wall and once again engage the shooter. During this shootout, the suspect was killed by police. The shooter had been interviewed at least twice by the FBI years prior to the deadly attack, but the FBI deemed him not to be a threat and was unable to take any criminal action against him.

International terrorism, that is, terrorist attacks that occur outside of the United States, provides further examples. On May 22, 2013, a British army soldier of the Royal Regiment of Fusiliers was walking on the street, off-duty, when he was attacked by two men. The two men ran him down with a car and then used knives and a cleaver to stab and hack him to death. One of the attackers even had the audacity to give an impromptu interview to a person in the area who was filming the carnage live, stating that they killed the soldier to avenge the killing of Muslims by British armed forces. The attackers remained at the scene until armed police arrived minutes later. The assailants charged at the police, who fired shots and wounded them both. The suspects were apprehended and taken to the hospital, where they both survived their gunshot wounds. The suspects were British men of Nigerian descent who were raised as Christians but had converted to Islam.

On September 21, 2013, around noon, at least four masked assailants attacked the upscale Westgate shopping mall in the Westland's district of Nairobi, Kenya. The gunmen reportedly carried assault rifles and wore combat fatigues. As they strolled through Westgate Mall, guns strapped to their torsos, the attackers chatted on their cell phones while they sprayed bullets at terrified shoppers. There were also reports of grenade explosions. Ruthless and nonchalant, they randomly gunned down shoppers. At one point, the shooters took turns to pray, removing shoes to perform the ritual washing in a room stacked with boxes. A man whimpering in a pool of blood on the floor crawled to get away. A gunman returned and shot him again. In between the gunfire, the attackers scanned ceilings for surveillance cameras. Nearby, shoppers hid behind cash registers while some ran for their lives. Others, too terrified to move, cowered on bloody floors. In addition to the two attackers in the supermarket, video surveillance footage shows two more shooters making their way through the parking lot. As they opened fire, shoppers slithered under cars for protection. Others tumbled to the ground, felled by bullets. The attackers in the parking lot later joined the others in the mall. Some of the shooters rounded up hostages. The terrorist attack lasted for four days and left at least sixty-seven people dead, many more injured, and dozens unaccounted for. The Al-Shabaab terrorist group (the largest of several armed Somali groups) claimed responsibility for the attacks.

On October 22, 2014, in Ottawa, Canada, an attacker ambushed two honor guard members on ceremonial guard duty at the Canadian National War Memorial, shooting and killing one of them. Fleeing the scene, the armed suspect ultimately entered Canada's Parliament with the intention of continuing his deadly rampage. At one point, shots were fired just outside the room where the Canadian Prime Minister was located. Security personnel, fearing that the Prime Minister might be harmed, instructed him to hide in a closet inside the room. Other occupants of the room had removed the flagpoles, broken them in half, and converted them into makeshift spears. The gunman was ultimately confronted by the sergeant at arms, who was armed with a handgun and reportedly shot the suspect at that location. The attacker had arrived in Canada in early October 2014 and was in Ottawa to deal with a passport issue, as he reportedly wanted to travel to Syria. The suspect had visited the United States at least four separate times in recent years.

On December 16, 2014, in Peshawar, Pakistan, the Taliban's Tariq Gedar group murdered 145 people at a public school. Included in the 145 victims were 132 school children. The Pakistani Taliban attacked the school because it was a public school that educated the children of the Pakistan army, and they wanted to strike out at the Pakistan army. The shooters in this school massacre consisted of seven terrorists who were armed with firearms and suicide vests. The killers meticulously went from room to room in search of and killing their intended targets—school children and their educators.

On April 2, 2015, terrorists from Somalia (Al-Shabaab) entered Garissa University College in Kenya, Africa, where they shot 147 people to death. The siege lasted for hours, and the gunmen reportedly separated people based on religion, shooting Christians and allowing Muslims to leave. Government security forces were able to respond and, as a result, four terrorists were killed.

In Istanbul, Turkey, three active shooters with suicide bombs attacked the airport on June 28, 2016. The terrorists approached three different areas of the airport and used their semi-automatic weapons to shoot innocent civilian passengers both inside and outside of the airport. After police engaged and shot one of the armed terrorists, the suspect fell to the ground and then purposely detonated the bomb he was carrying. All three of the terrorists detonated their bombs, killing themselves along with numerous innocent people. The death toll was forty-four, with over 140 injured.

And again during a 2017 New Year's Eve celebration, an upscale nightclub in Istanbul, Turkey saw yet another terrorist attack. A gunman shot and killed one police officer stationed outside a nightclub and entered the club. The gunman using an assault rifle killed at least 39 people and wounded another 69. During the rampage, the gunman stopped shooting long enough to change magazines at least five times. After the shooting, the gunman changed clothing before fleeing the scene.

Although these terrorist attacks did not occur inside the United States, ask yourself: If this were to happen in any of our shopping malls, airports, nightclubs or college campuses, are any of us are truly prepared to deal with such an event? There is no question that the United States could have one or more domestic or foreign terrorists that are motivated to pose the same deadly threat as the ones that occurred in Oslo, Norway, Istanbul, Turkey and Mumbai, India.

Desensitization regarding human life has been argued to be a product of the graphic violence found in modern American culture. With the introduction of technology into our daily lives, some people's craving for stimulus appears unquenchable. The movies and TV shows that depict supernatural monsters or glorified violent attacks give some people nightmares, while others derive pleasure from seeing such carnage. Major motion pictures depict average people who are beaten down by the system and exact revenge on those whom they feel are responsible. Whether the victims of their injustices truly had it coming or were in the wrong places at the wrong times, the results were a number of felonious assaults, shootings, and other violent attacks, all meant to obtain the maximum visual effect. Some viewers may be able to differentiate between fantasy and reality and realize they have just watched a movie. However, some people may not be capable of that differentiation and will use that movie as a guide and justification for their future acts of carnage.

In March of 2014, a prime time TV series depicted cult followers entering a public place and stabbing patrons with knives. On April

9, 2014, in Murrysville, Pennsylvania, over twenty high school students were stabbed by one of their own classmates. The assailant, a sophomore male armed with at least two knives, went on a thirty-minute rampage throughout the school, moving from classroom to classroom as he continuously stabbed his fellow students. Although there were school resource officers present at the school at the time of the attack, the high school assistant principal and another student are credited with stopping the attack and facilitating the apprehension of the student. Whether the suspect in the stabbing at Murrysville High School had watched this particular TV show or the knife attack was just a coincidence, only the attacker knows for sure.

Video games have also evolved from fairly abstract and nonviolent games to graphic first-person shooters of supernatural monsters and other human beings. These games are not only available on desktop computers, but can be played on consoles, cell phones, and tablet computers at whim. Many games can be played online so that different players can compete against each other. The types of "video crimes" that players engage in include, but are not limited to, robbery, carjacking, shooting, rape, and vehicular homicide against other characters in the game.

Video arcades also have violent games where a player can physically hold a replica firearm (pistol, shotgun, or semi-automatic weapon) to shoot virtual opponents. The way in which individuals handle these replica weapons is reminiscent of the techniques and demeanor typically seen in police or military settings. If the players are not imitating those types of firearms techniques, they imitate the gangster style of shooter, holding the pistol sideways as they shoot at the screen. These people, who may never have had any real experience in weapons handling, are quickly learning how to stand, hold a gun, shoot, and engage multiple targets within these violent games.

One needs to consider the effect of video game, TV, and movie portrayals of violence on impressionable individuals who may be inspired to imitate the act(s) seen on the screen. One could easily make the case of life imitating art in several active shooter/assailant cases. Contemporary technology has lulled responsible parents, young adults, and children into some type of hypnotic state where they do not hold as much regard for human life.

In the past, games and movies were purchased inside a store. If the content was too demeaning toward women or too vulgar, there was a parental advisory to ensure that youth were unable to easily obtain such material. Now, material that degrades women and people of color and glorifies violent acts can be downloaded regardless of parental oversight. Does this audio-visual degradation provide some impressionable individuals with the idea that what they are hearing and seeing is cool and can be done to whomever they want without any consequences? While sociologists and psychiatrists can debate these types of issues for some time, the shootings and killings that are almost at epidemic proportions seem to continue unabated.

Shooter's Mentality and Demeanor

In a *spontaneous event,* something will spark the flame of violence within the assailant, who responds with a violent action that occurs within moments of the aggravating igniting factor. On September 26, 2014, in Moore, Oklahoma, a male suspect had recently been suspended at his job. The employee left the building and returned minutes later and attacked two women with an eight-inch kitchen knife. The COO of the company (who is also a reserve deputy) shot the suspect.

In a *premeditated event,* the offended person has decided to embark upon a violent course of conduct and will plan accordingly. This violent act can occur hours, days, weeks, months, or even years after the igniting factor. The premeditated shooter will go through several mental and physical phases prior to committing a crime. They will choose to appear on the day, time, and location of the shooting and will bring the weapons to be used during their rampage. Those who elect to shoot, stab, or otherwise kill people in public and private places will experience and move though a progression of violent behavior. These people committing mass murders do not suddenly snap and go on a violent shooting rampage.

Phases of an Active Shooter

The shooter will move through a series of stages that result finally in violent and deadly actions. The progression consists of four distinct phases. The active shooter will transition though these phases prior to any premeditated act of violence. These shootings are premeditated, and there is no element of coincidence in that they have all their weapons and ammunition with them at the time they begin shooting. These phases can take place anywhere from days to years before the assailant arrives at their chosen destination to begin their deadly rampage.

Grievance: This is where the assailant is upset over a particular issue. This could be some real or perceived area where they felt wronged, ranging from relationship issues to work disputes or revengeful obsession.

Ideation and Fantasy: The assailant somehow comes upon the idea that the method chosen to resolve their grievance is to use a firearm or other deadly weapons in order to kill those whom they believe had somehow hurt them. In some cases, the assailant has communicated this fantasy via social media.

Research, plan, and prepare: The assailant will think, conduct research, plan, and prepare for the deadly attack. In this phase, the shooter/assailant may plan (and in some cases write) in detail the location, date, and time of the attack and obtain all of the items they will need (such as firearms, ammunition, other weapons, or an IED).

Implementation: This is when the assailant has elected to execute the plan. They will approach the location, enter — with their weapon either in full view or concealed—and begin their deadly rampage. A shooter who enters the location with their weapon already in full view may elect to shoot targets of opportunity that they come across or wait to meet the target that has been selected for termination. When the assailant has chosen to conceal their firearms, they will have been hidden using a variety of methods, such as backpacks, guitar cases, briefcases, or on their person. These assailants will usually conceal their weapon successfully, enter the facility or grounds, and, once inside, choose the time and the place to remove their weapon(s) and begin shooting and killing people. In the June 2015 Charleston, South Carolina, church shooting, the shooter entered the church and participated in the Bible study for over an hour before he decided to implement his murderous rampage. In other cases, the shooter has approached and entered the facility with their primary weapon in full view of everyone.

Some may believe that only a crazy person can commit such violent acts against innocent people. Whatever causes these people to have their "psychotic episodes" is immaterial. What is important is to understand that innocent people will always be their victims.

Research into nearly any completed pre-meditated shooting will eventually show that the shooter has transitioned through these four phases. Once the potential shooter has begun these phases, unless information is discovered that exposes their deadly plot, the killing event will be extremely difficult to stop.

The demeanor of the shooters may vary during the actual shooting. Watching the video surveillance of the Columbine High School shooters, one sees the two shooters mocking and laughing at their victims as they stalk them through the school. Even as the victims were screaming and practically begging for their lives, the shooters showed no compassion. In watching the video footage of the 2010 Florida School Board shooting, one can see that the shooters appeared very angry and focused. A woman attempted to knock the handgun out of one of the shooter's hand but was unsuccessful. It was clear that the shooter had chosen his targets for the shooting, and this woman was not one of them. Although one of the members of the board attempted to negotiate with the shooter, he was still determined that someone was going to die that day.

In order to prevent any shooting event from occurring, especially during any of the phases prior to the implementation of the shooting, one would have to be aware of what the potential shooter is personally experiencing. Coworkers, family, and friends play an integral role in being aware of the events in the potential shooter's life with the hope of identifying their troubles (or illness) and stopping them during their progression prior to the implementation of the deadly event. These people would need to be privy to threatening statements the potential shooter may have made, and any social media rants. They may also be aware of the shooter's preparation, particularly the process of gathering weapons or ammunition.

In the aftermath of numerous shooting cases, it was apparent that friends, parents, coworkers, supervisors, and other authority figures had some hint of the potential for harm, either from something the shooter said prior to the event or through social media posts. They either failed to pick up on these clues or failed to mention such bizarre behavior, such as the gathering of weapons, to others. In other cases, the authority figures were given advance warning of the threat and either failed to recognize the clues, failed to act, or failed to take the necessary steps that perhaps could have intervened to stop the shooting prior to the actual event.

Shooters typically seek specific targets for their deadly rampages. The shooter may select targets based on a person, company, or location. In the case of a workplace shooting, the shooter may seek out specific or random managers within the company. Sometimes, specific coworkers are chosen. If those specific targets are unavailable, the shooter may accept targets of opportunity. That is when others within the kill zone are in the most danger. In shootings where the killer moves about killing indiscriminately, the shooter may accept every person as a target of opportunity. During the shooting, the shooter may feel more empowered with each shot fired toward a human target.

A shooter who has located and shot the intended target(s) has been known to stop shooting and end the armed assault. In other cases, they have continued shooting other victims within the kill zone and will only stop the shooting spree when successfully challenged. At that time, they sometimes choose to shoot and kill themselves.

The shooter is more likely to be armed with more than one firearm and/or have additional ammunition for the weapon(s). In past cases, the range of weapons has been a combination of handguns, long guns, knives, and improvised explosive devices. Once the shooter has engaged targets with their primary weapon, the shooter may reload that weapon or discard it for another deadly weapon. Nearly every case illustrates this point.

The shooter in the July 20, 2012, massacre in a crowded movie theater in Aurora, Colorado, was carrying a variety of firearms and gas grenades. The shooter wore a gas mask, a ballistic helmet, and a vest with leg, groin, and throat protectors. He used a gas grenade, an AR-15 military-style semi-automatic rifle, a shotgun, and two pistols, killing twelve people and injuring sixty others during his rampage. The suspect was arrested near his car, which was parked behind the theater, while still carrying three weapons.

On February 20, 2014, in Cedarville, California, at Cedarville Rancheria, a Native American tribal office, a former tribal leader was at a hearing because she was facing eviction. She suddenly began shooting, and when she ran out of ammunition, she grabbed a butcher knife from the kitchen and stabbed another person. Four people were killed, and two others were injured. A person at the meeting ran out of the building covered in blood and went to the Alturas police station to alert officers. When police responded to the scene, they found the female suspect outside the building, running with a knife in her hands. The assailant was taken into custody.

Once the killing event starts, the assailant expresses a desire to kill and seriously injure others without concern for his/her own safety. Negotiating with the shooter has only worked in a few cases, and I would not recommend this tactic. The shooter will continue to move through the area shooting and killing people until someone stops the killing or the shooter decides to stop. Oftentimes, the shooter does not have an escape plan and may elect to end their life, either after shooting and killing their chosen targets, or when it becomes apparent that law enforcement is responding to the shooting, on scene, or when they engage the shooter. The shooter is not only homicidal, but suicidal as well. Perhaps past shooters may have heard the sounds of the approaching law enforcement via their blaring sirens, or when police have entered the premises and confronted the assailants. Other times, when confronted by competent intervention (police intervention or armed security who engaged the suspect with gunfire), the shooter has elected that moment to end their own life by gunfire.

Shooting locations

Shootings and mass killings have occurred in a variety of places across the United States, including churches, public and private workplaces, museums, police stations, subway trains, casinos, fast-food restaurants, hospitals, shopping malls, public and private schools, and college campuses. A comprehensive list of all the locations where such events have occurred would fill many pages, as active shooters have chosen a host of locations in which they can inflict deadly consequences on their largely unsuspecting victims. The locations chosen are based solely on the shooter's motivation and choice of victims.

The choice of locations can also be contingent on the rationale (or illogical ideas) of the shooter. The shooter may be looking to exact revenge on a particular person or group. They may also choose a location because it will provide the greatest number of casualties or the most extensive media coverage for the deadly event.

Soft targets are places that have little to no resistance or apparent plan to observe, stop, intervene, or effectively mitigate an active shooter/assailant. An example is the typical work environment of an office building. In these situations, a receptionist will usually greet the visitor and notify the party that needs to be seen, advising the visitor to take a seat and wait. The door that leads from the reception desk to the office areas is often glass and is rarely secured in any fashion that prevents unwanted entry. Consider a church, a school, a fast-food restaurant, or a movie theater. On July 23, 2015, at a movie theater in Lafayette, Louisiana, a single adult stood up twenty minutes into the movie and shot and killed two women before turning the gun on himself.

Shooters may choose those "soft target" locations because, in their evaluation, it lacks people who possess the knowledge, skills, expertise, and armed capability to effectively address their deadly rampages. As people all over the world continue to leave their homes, live their lives, go to work, school, or places of worship, and frequent public places, any of those places may have been or will be surreptitiously selected by the active shooter as the exact place for their particular shooting.

Hard targets are buildings that are known to always have a contingency of armed personnel, such as a police department, a courthouse, and some museums. These locations usually have secured their entry and exit locations with gates, secure doors, and fortified front lobby areas where the public enters through metal detectors. A large number of people within that building are armed and typically well-versed on how to respond should an armed person suddenly appear and start shooting. Although the majority of shooters have chosen "soft targets" for their event, there are examples of shooters who purposely walk into places where armed personnel are known to be present and still manage to ambush unsuspecting, armed individuals.

On January 6, 2010, the Washington, DC, Holocaust Museum was the scene of a shooting. At about 12:49 p.m., the eighty-eight-year-old suspect drove his car to the entrance of the museum. The suspect entered the museum, and when a museum special police officer opened the door for him, the suspect raised a .22-caliber rifle and shot the officer. Two other special police officers stationed at that location returned fire, wounding the suspect.

On April 7, 2014, a man opened fire at the front desk of a Los Angeles Police Department building. The shooting occurred around eight o'clock p.m. at the LAPD Wilshire Division and West Traffic Division office. The suspect entered the lobby and opened fire. Officers returned fire, striking the suspect. The shooter was taken to the hospital. One of the officers was shot seven times by the suspect and survived.

The potential motivation of the shooter to choose one location over another could be due to seeking specific victims. An example is that of a workplace violence act where the shooter returns to the site of their former employment. It could also be due to a domestic incident that has gone terribly wrong. The estranged half of the couple may have appeared at the other half's place of work, place of worship, grocery store, and many other locations seeking out the person they want to do the most harm to. Many parents who have some type of custody agreement are sometimes routed to a public place to exchange their children into the other parent's custody. For the parent who may have decided on using a firearm against a former significant other, those public places could become a very public killing zone.

Shooters Who Escaped from the Initial Shooting Location

There are cases where shooters have escaped from the initial shooting scene and either turned themselves in to police, been captured after an extensive manhunt, or been confronted by law enforcement officers and killed. It should be noted that as these types of mass shootings continue to occur, shooters have evolved in their tactics, including escaping from the initial crime scene. Shooters rarely escape from a shooting scene and fade away into total obscurity.

On April 12, 2012, in Oakland, California, seven people were killed and three others wounded in a shooting rampage at an Asian religious vocational school. The gunman, armed with a .45-caliber semi-automatic handgun with four fully loaded ten-round magazines, entered a classroom holding onto the school's receptionist, whom he had just taken hostage. The gunman ordered everyone to the front of the class and then began shooting anyone who entered. The suspect fled the scene in a victim's car before the police arrived and drove to a Safeway about five miles away. The suspect telephoned his father, who was able to persuade him to surrender. Once the police arrived, the shooter surrendered without further incident. The shooter was a nursing student who was no longer enrolled in the school, but it is unknown whether the shooter had dropped out or was expelled.

The Beltway sniper attacks in Washington, DC, Maryland, and Virginia occurred in 2002 over three weeks. After each shooting, the suspects were able to escape. Eventually, the two suspects involved were captured and prosecuted for their crimes. The one difference between this and other mass killings is the number of victims for each shooting event.

On October 5, 2011, a disgruntled employee of a rock quarry located in Cupertino, California, opened fire during an early morning safety meeting. After killing three coworkers and wounding six others, the suspect left the area and taunted his coworkers via radio. The suspect then attempted to carjack a vehicle and shot the driver of that vehicle. The suspect fled on foot from the area. The following day, police confronted a man who fit the physical description of the suspect in the neighboring city of Sunnyvale, California. After a threatening motion was made by the suspect, officers opened fire. It was later determined that the suspect actually died from a self-inflicted gunshot wound.

On June 17, 2015, the 180-year-old Emanuel African Methodist Episcopal Church located in downtown Charleston, South Carolina, was attacked by a single gunman. The shooting took place during an early evening prayer service, and it was reported that the gunman had been inside the church for over an hour prior to the shooting. A total of nine members of the church were killed. The mayor of Charleston advised during a press conference that the shootings were a hate crime based on the ethnicity of the assailant and his victims. The gunman spared one woman who was told to tell the world what had happened. After the killings, the gunman fled the scene only to be captured in Shelby, North Carolina, by law enforcement the following day.

On December 2, 2015, in San Bernardino, California, one man and his wife, wearing masks, body armor, and military-style clothing, entered Inland Regional Center, where a Christmas party was underway. The killers began shooting using semi-automatic rifles and killed at least fourteen people, wounding many others. They fled the scene prior to the arrival of any law enforcement personnel. The suspects' vehicle was later tracked by police, and the suspects engaged the police in gunfire and were killed.

Lastly, on September 23, 2016 a twenty year old man using a rifle shot and killed five people at a Macy's makeup counter at the Cascade Mall in Burlington, Washington. The shooter left the rifle and fled the scene but was ultimately identified and captured by police the following day.

Part 2

Dynamics That Facilitate an Active Shooter Event

....

Organizational officials should continuously take proactive steps to appropriately train all their personnel on all relevant factors and defense strategies against an active shooter/assailant. All employees need to know and observe the warning signs of potentially violent individuals within their work environment and be fully educated on internally and externally based threats for an active shooter/assailant. Any organization that is aware of a potential violent situation/problem and fails to take timely action is putting its personnel directly and indirectly in harm's way. All employees need to be educated on how to appropriately mitigate an active shooter/assailant event, covering the full range of options, including escaping the kill zone, sheltering to hide, and tactical and practical defensive techniques for their survival when they must shelter and fight.

When any organization knows of the threats, yet fails to take these steps for their own personnel, they may be held liable for subsequent litigation. Some of the questions that will ultimately arise when litigation does occur are:

1. What did management officials know about the threat?
2. When did management officials first learn of the threat?
3. What, within reason, did management officials do to mitigate the threat?

Signs Restricting Weapons

There are locations that restrict the use or presence of weapons (firearms) on their premises. Legally armed citizens are advised via signs posted near the entrances of the facility not to bring their concealed or open-carry weapons inside. This discussion will cover private businesses (not city, state, or federal properties) where it is not against the law to possess a firearm but where the business has decided that they want a gun-free zone. As an example, a sign clearly posted on the front of a department store may advise, "No concealed weapons." Some signs may add "by order of state law," which indicates that the presence of guns on this facility is prohibited by law, rather than at the discretion of the facility. I do not advocate breaking the law. You should research local laws concerning carrying firearms into private locations to ensure that you are not breaking any laws. When in doubt, don't break the law.

Remember, potential customers can choose whether to patronize or not patronize your business on the basis of that prohibition. They can always choose to ignore your private sign and bring their weapon inside. Your policy does not have the same legal force as state law. This is a decision that legally armed citizens must make for themselves, after considering the consequences of having or not having their firearms, even though a private venue says otherwise.

In the 1991 Luby's Cafeteria shooting, the assailant approached one restaurant patron and her parents. As the restaurant patron reached for the .38 revolver in her purse, she remembered she had left it in her vehicle to comply with the law, which at the time stated that concealed carry was not allowed in "public places." The patron's father, a seventy-one-year-old man, rushed at the shooter in an attempt to subdue him, but was fatally shot in the chest.

Instead of forbidding firearms to be carried on a property, these locations should prominently display signs that warn any potential shooter that persons within this area are legally armed and that possession of the defender's handgun is welcomed. It would be interesting to note how many "soft targets" would still be vulnerable if the average law-abiding citizen were welcome to carry a legally possessed and concealed firearm.

Preemptive Facility Measures

Access control can be used to delay entry of a potential shooter and, in some cases, even deny access. The fortification of entry locations for some facilities and schools has recently occurred in numerous places throughout the country. Specifically, school districts have implemented the "single point of entry" approach. This concept funnels anyone who enters the school (during school hours) to the main office. The exterior portions of the school are fenced off, and the exterior doors are locked to prevent unwanted entry into the school or onto the school grounds.

Fortifying the front doors is thought to be one way to make it more difficult for an active shooter to gain entry. This method may slow down the potential shooter. However, if this is the only or most significant method of prevention, it is, at its best, only a small step to deal with both the internally and externally based threats. This approach assumes that the shooter will follow the rules and approach the school via the fortified entrance. Secondly, it assumes the shooter will come to the school's front door only after all the students have entered the school and the front doors have been secured. Some school officials have only grasped one piece of a huge array of items to bolster school safety. This answer falls way short of any true attempt to address the school shooter.

The single point of entry was in place during the school shooting in Newtown, Connecticut; however, the externally based shooter merely shot through the glass and entered the school. Once inside the school, the shooter killed twenty-six people before he took his own life. The single point of entry was also in place at Sparks Middle School in Sparks, Nevada. In that case, the internally based shooter came onto school property via the rear of the school playground area prior to the start of school. The shooter produced a handgun and shot two students. One teacher was killed. The shooter then turned the gun on himself and took his own life.

How much money nationwide has been spent on this effort, which only provides a false sense of security to parents, teachers, and students?

Law Enforcement Response to the Active Shooter Scene

Prior to the Columbine school shooting, standard protocol for active shootings was for officers to quickly arrive on the scene, set up a perimeter, contain the scene, and then call and wait for the arrival of SWAT personnel to resolve the situation. In the Columbine case, the shooters continued to shoot and kill innocent people, roaming freely inside the kill zone, while SWAT personnel were arriving and deploying into position. Law enforcement nationwide realized that they could no longer use this traditional emergency response.

Law enforcement agencies all over the United States have devoted exorbitant amounts of time and effort to train their police personnel on how to respond to an active shooter, specifically how to apply force to ultimately resolve the deadly threat to the victims of that location. The contemporary response is for law enforcement to arrive and immediately enter the scene, searching for and engaging the shooter.

Although this current response is hailed as a much better tactic to save lives, when seconds count, the police are still minutes away.

This is not a condemnation of any law enforcement agency, merely stating that no one should just sit and wait for law enforcement to solve the issue. Response times indicate that it can literally take minutes for police to arrive. The average response time for the first officers to arrive on the scene of a shooting can be anywhere from one to three minutes. During that time, the potential victims are left to deal with an armed assailant. The shooter may be searching for a specific target or may just want to kill anyone and everyone that comes across their path. Those who are still inside the kill zone are forced to deal with the deadly threat until the police arrive, when the shooter either commits suicide or is shot/captured by law enforcement personnel.

Photographs from active shootings show that, once the police have responded, the response is overwhelming. Officers from a variety of different law enforcement agencies will respond to address the threat. The scene will be chaotic, and communication issues between police agencies will be a constant problem as they attempt to mitigate the active shooter. From a middle school shooting in Sparks, Nevada, it was reported that over 200 police officers from a variety of different agencies responded to the scene of the shooting, some from more than sixty miles away. However, this takes time, and you cannot always afford the luxury of waiting for them to save your life.

Empowering citizens is an untapped mitigation factor for addressing the active shooter, and this book seeks to tap into that resource. Our citizens need to feel safe and empowered and know that their observations and concerns will be heard, addressed, and resolved in a timely fashion. Citizens need to see that when authorities are notified, appropriate steps are taken to stop the threat and intervene with the potential shooter before the event occurs. However, many cases have illustrated that authorities are often incapable of taking all the actions necessary to enhance our safety.

In sharp contrast to empowering citizens and in their haste to reduce mass shootings, some jurisdictions have passed laws or regulations restricting areas where firearms may be possessed by individuals who are otherwise legally allowed to carry concealed weapons. Although the issue of gun control will likely be debated for some time, it is a simple fact that if potential victims had legal firearms in their possession and the mental capacity to take action, the body count in many shootings would be significantly less. By banning weapons within those locations, authorities effectively disarm law-abiding citizens, who are left with no effective means to counter the deadly threat of an armed assailant. These gun-free zones have effectively been turned into "murder magnets."

Contemporary strategies used by many law enforcement agencies require the victims to place their safety in the hands of law enforcement officers who will ultimately respond and arrive at the scene to address the deadly force threat. The victims are required to submit total control of their lives to someone else, who they only hope and pray will get there in time to save their lives. However, a shooter who has begun to engage the targets of their rampage will continue to move through the area and to kill innocent people until competent intervention occurs that stops the shooter. In any threat environment, do whatever you can to keep as much control over your own safety as possible, without relinquishing absolute power to anyone. Take into account that you may only have a matter of seconds to make a decision. You alone may be the one who is actually present and dealing with the armed assailant.

An example where armed personnel on the scene of an active shooting effectively intervened occurred on December 16, 2012. A man upset over the breakup of his relationship showed up at his girlfriend's place of work. The shooter pulled out a gun and attempted to open fire in the restaurant, but his weapon jammed. The patrons and employees of the restaurant escaped the building. The shooter chased the employees into a nearby movie theater and continued his rampage. An off-duty sergeant, who was working security, heard the gunshots and saw the gunman coming out of the men's restroom. The off-duty sergeant shot the gunman four times. Only one other person was wounded, a forty-nine-year-old man inside the theater. According to report, approximately thirty rounds were fired by the gunman.

Past shooters have repeatedly demonstrated that they will not be hampered by laws, rules, or signs that prohibit the possession of firearms within an establishment. Past cases have also shown that these shooters have taken a variety of guns, explosives, and other deadly weapons into these areas with the intention to harm, maim, and kill innocent people within that gun-free zone.

Some authorities are not yet ready to shift their approach and consider that people have a right to defend themselves. Banning the possession of firearms by the "good guys" is not the best way to resolve or address the threat of an active shooter. The one sure method for stopping a bad guy with a gun who is in the process of shooting and killing innocent people is a good guy with a gun who possesses the knowledge, skills, and mindset to apply the appropriate force. People who have firearms readily accessible to defend themselves should never be restricted based on the location and the fact that these shootings have occurred within those same gun-free zones.

Reactive Personal Measures

When in any public or private place, typically outside your own personal residence, remain vigilant for signs of extreme disturbances and for dangerous people who live among us. While addressing the enormous issues surrounding an active shooter, we must use a multi-faceted approach to safety to educate each and every person in the workforce on how to effectively mitigate an active shooter rather than simply fortifying the exterior of buildings and training law enforcement, who can do nothing until they arrive on the scene.

Information should be viewed as a toolbox. While some tools may prove useful, other tools may not only be totally useless, but dangerous to employ in a deadly situation. Every community deserves to have its schools, businesses, and places of worship adequately protected and to be provided with true lifesaving measures against potential threats.

On the heels of the Columbine school shootings, I, along with several law enforcement officials, met with officials within a school district and illustrated an in-depth training program which we then proposed for the entire district. The superintendent of the school sent me a nice letter thanking me for the program and stated that he hoped they would never have to use it. Only a small part of my recommendations were ever implemented. None of those were the integral portions that instructed educators and administrators how to protect their students against an active shooter. When attempting to address the threat of a mass shooting inside a local mall following the massacre in Nairobi, Kenya, I communicated with mall officials to propose training for their employees. The management's response was that they didn't allow people outside our organization to provide training. Therefore, no training occurred, and employees can only pray that no shooting ever occurs in their areas.

More can always be done to address the significant threat of an active shooter, and so far, the majority of our valuable and dwindling resources have been focused toward target hardening, increased law enforcement training, and short training sessions for targeted audiences that teach extremely ineffective solutions to a very complex problem. Although law enforcement has dedicated significant time and resources to training their people on how to respond to an active shooting, they still fail to devote any time or effort to teach the real victims. They fail to adequately teach people how to run, where to run, where to hide, and more importantly, how to tactically and technically fight an armed assailant.

Shooters are not deterred from entering into their intended locations. In fact, I am unaware of any shooter who was turned back by the gun-free zones and fortified doors, or even by heavy security or police presence. The shooters appear to have still gone into those places, even if only in that area before the metal detectors, and committed their acts of violence.

On July 24, 1998, officers were assigned to operate the X-ray machine and magnetometer at the document door entrance on the east front of the US Capitol Building. A male suspect, armed with a .38 caliber handgun, entered the document door at 3:40 p.m. As one officer was providing directions to a tourist and his son, his partner was escorting another tourist toward the restroom. The suspect entered the area and walked around the metal detector just inside the entrance. The suspect was directed to go back through the metal detector. Instead, the suspect produced a gun and without warning shot the first officer in the back of the head. The suspect walked down a short corridor and pushed through a door leading to a group of offices used by senior Republican representatives. One of the plainclothes detectives was shot after the suspect entered one of the offices. Despite being mortally wounded, the detective was able to return fire and wound the suspect, who was apprehended in that office. A female tourist suffered minor injuries after bullets grazed her shoulder and face.

This example clearly illustrates a shooter who is not deterred by armed law enforcement or an armed security presence. The suspect was still bent on entering the facility and shooting and killing anyone he chose. Those people in influential positions should recognize that it's about the good of the people, not about them. It should always be about how we can work together with whoever has qualified information on this subject in order to save lives.

Most government officials should swear an oath that it's not only their job, but also their duty to protect those within their area of responsibility. Leaders who are unable or unwilling to do what is required to mitigate a deadly threat should remove the obstacles and allow others to provide valuable and timely training for the targeted population. These leaders should never tie the hands of those innocent people who clearly need to help themselves.

Police can never be everywhere, and no one should have to depend 100 percent on someone else for their safety. What is needed is for people to be taught how to fight effectively when their lives depend on it. When people are in a confined space and are forced to defend themselves, allow them to have access to all the tools, strategies, tactics, and techniques necessary to survive a deadly threat. Leaders need to educate and empower people, not restrict them.

On December 7, 1993, on a Long Island commuter train, a shooter pulled out his gun and started shooting fellow passengers. He killed six and wounded nineteen before being stopped by three of the passengers, who acted to save their lives as well as the lives of others.

The airline industry is an example of how this paradigm can change. Historically, specifically prior to 9/11, the policy for aircraft hijacking was for the crew and passengers to cooperate with the hijackers so that everything could be resolved without the loss of life. The US government would ultimately use their resources to get the aircraft, crew, and passengers back to the United States with everyone safe and sound. But 9/11 changed all of that. The passengers aboard United Airlines Flight 93 used items within their environment as improvised weapons and fought the terrorist to save additional lives. Since then, passengers aboard aircraft have been inspired to violently resist any threat to the aircraft that endangers their lives.

In one case from January 4, 2013, a passenger aboard a flight from Iceland to New York City became unruly and violent after he consumed a bottle of alcohol. The violent passenger choked another passenger and said that the plane was going to crash. Other passengers aboard the plane intervened and subdued the violent passenger. The unruly passenger was restrained and confined to his seat by duct tape and plastic zip ties. The intervention of passengers to effectively deal with a violent threat aboard an aircraft is not the first and certainly will not be the last. Passengers have realized that the law enforcement officials tasked with the responsibility to address such threats (federal air marshals) cannot be on every flight. These passengers have decided that they will use whatever means they have to ensure their safety.

Officials need to make allowances and allow for flexibility for all law-abiding citizens to take an active role in protecting their own lives and, in doing so, directly or indirectly potentially saving the lives of others.

Supervision Issues

When a particular industry, organization, or location has had one or more active shooting events, the style of management needs to be closely scrutinized. It needs to be recognized that good workers do not automatically become good supervisors Supervising employees is no easy job! Rarely are supervisors provided with the training necessary to become great supervisors, nor are they afforded the time necessary to know and understand what motivates every worker.

It could be inferred that the sheer number of shootings at United States postal facilities was due to poor management. Postal managers were reportedly rude and mean to their employees, often bullying them. Several long-term postal employees reported that the management and supervision practices had not changed since the earliest reports of shooting at postal facilities. One employee from northern Nevada stated that if it wasn't for bad management, we'd have no management at all. Another employee of the postal service in southern California revealed that supervisors are often promoted not on merit, but on favoritism. Once these individuals are promoted, the organizational culture is to really push the employees to get the mail out faster. It was also stated there is still a great deal of disrespect shown by some supervisors toward employees and that yelling at employees is a common practice.

There is also a potential issue with younger employees who were raised in homes in which holding individuals accountable and responsible was not common. These employees are now in a workforce that is very demanding and sometimes insulting. These young employees rebel against the older, established supervisors. This rebellion may light the spark that results in a potentially disruptive confrontation in the future.

When an employee appears to have a problem at work, the typical workplace is more interested in productivity than in helping that employee solve their problems, whether personal or professional. Most large companies take the "cookie-cutter" approach to address and resolve all work problems. Some supervisors and managers may not be as competent as their job really requires. Merely passing a promotional test does not guarantee that a new supervisor is truly the best person for the job. The supervisor needs to work to resolve problems appropriately and in a timely fashion, to encourage the best performance of each worker, and to deal effectively with those who do not (or will not) complete their work. To this end, the supervisor may need to make courageous and sometimes unpopular decisions. The rewarding of good employees and holding errant employees accountable are parts of being a supervisor. Supervisors need to be educated on how to supervise and to appropriately motivate employees. Some supervisors and managers resort to bullying their employees and appear not to care about an employee's personal needs.

If the primary targets of a workplace shooting are the managers and supervisors, what does it say about their management style or the culture of the organization? If the leadership style of their supervisors is what sparked the troubled employee, and a workplace shooting does occur, did the workplace learn from that event? Are they still managing people through intimidation and fear?

Ineffective Active Shooter Training

Various law enforcement agencies have compiled copious amounts of information and analysis of nearly every aspect of the active shooter.

Listing the locations of where the shootings have taken place, the reasons the shooter committed his/her rampage, and the methods chosen by the shooter to conceal his/her weapon forms the bulk of this analysis. While this information is important to know and can provide critical insight about active shooters, one should not get caught up in statistics regarding the average ages, genders, and nationalities of shooters.

Law enforcement nationwide has spent hundreds of hours training SWAT teams and their patrol officers on the tactics to use when responding to an active shooter/assailant. Officers are trained to arrive on scene, link up with additional law enforcement personnel, and enter the facility in search of the assailant. Officers are not trained to confront assailants with the intent to apprehend them. Officers are trained to address the threat with deadly force and to stop the immediate loss of innocent lives. School district law enforcement has provided training in the form of a video advocating the current industry response of run, hide, and fight. Every school district employee is mandated to watch the video presentation.

Every person within an active shooter/assailant environment should have a thorough understanding of the assailant and the complexities of the attack coupled with tactical information and physical techniques to expeditiously mitigate the threat. Officials need to be aware of civil litigation that comes out of failure to train. After a shooting, a judge will determine who knew what, when they knew it, what they did about it, and thus who is liable for allowing, facilitating, or not acting to prevent such events. Expert witnesses will be summoned. Courts have found organizations liable when it can be demonstrated that they failed to properly protect those under their care. Officials should be prepared to write large checks to pay for their negligent, generic, and ineffective training techniques. Instead of providing crucial information and training, active shooter training falls into several pitfall and problem categories.

Barriers to Active Shooter/Assailant Defense Training

There are a number of intentional, active, and purposeful hindrances involved in proactive defense training. What I have found is alarming, shocking, and occasionally downright despicable. These interferences with providing proactive training can be a company's posture, approach, perspective, or general attitude toward training.

Ostrich Approach/Reaction

Sticking your head in the ground and ignoring the problem is never a plausible method to address any threat. This approach will ultimately come back to bite those who participate in this approach/reaction. At a major office complex in southern California, when asked about their active shooter defense training program, a plainclothes security officer stated that he often wondered what he would do because his security firm had never educated him on what he should do. The security director for that complex stated they already had all the training they needed and all their personnel had already been trained. Perhaps someone failed to pass along that training information to all their staff members, who more than likely will be the ones patrons and employees of that complex look to during a shooting event.

Gatekeeper Obstruction

Gatekeepers are individuals within an organization who stop everything at their front door. They feel their people already possess all the knowledge, skills, and abilities to deal with an active shooter/assailant threat and they don't need or want, nor will they accept, outside help. These gatekeepers feel their empire is being challenged and fear that, by allowing outside information, their image or authority might be diminished in the eyes of those within their organization who hold them in such high esteem. In some cases, it could be that they write and believe their own press. Perhaps they feel that they have promoted them to the status of premier authority on the subject and therefore no one can teach them anything. For them, the thought that people outside their organization could provide anything that could remotely help the real victims of a shooting will only fall on deaf ears. The result of these gatekeepers is organizational bureaucratic paralysis, which directly affects and threatens the safety of the people they are supposed to protect and serve.

One of many examples of this barrier comes from a presentation done for active shooter/assailant defense in Nevada for the top two officials in their school police department (a chief and the sergeant responsible for active shooter training). Throughout the presentation, these two officials were argumentative and self-righteous, constantly looking at their cell phones as if they had better things to do. After I demonstrated with one school official how an individual could simply disarm a shooter armed with a handgun, the chief indicated that he would never teach that tactic to anyone because, in his training experiences, the defender was never successful and would always be injured during the disarming effort. When I contested the effectiveness of the disarming strategy, the chief responded with the objection that the technique was useless if the shooter was left-handed, despite my assertions to the contrary. The sergeant indicated that he believed teaching mental preparation was the best use of their time. Despite his apparent knowledge about past shooting incidents in schools, when I asked whether he had any alternative or practical strategies for an individual to defend themselves against an assailant, the chief was silent.

While people in positions of authority sit back and debate the merits of teaching others to fight back or not, they are in the safety and comfort of their offices and have the luxury of being legally armed within their environment. In contrast, the majority of the people whom they are sworn to protect are unarmed and are dependent on what these individuals allow to filter down to them. Neither of these two arrogant individuals possessed any of the qualifications or expertise in physical tactics to be capable of forming any reasonable and legitimate opinion to critique a physical technique. Nor could these two provide any techniques or tactics other than to hide from the shooter/assailant and wait for the armed on-duty police to arrive. This is a prime example of not doing anything to help the people that need help the most. They refuse to have others come into or onto their "turf" to help, yet they don't provide any advice other than to run and hide from the shooter/assailant.

Building Lock Out Defense

A number of schools and other entities have embraced the concept of a single point of entry to address the threat. Locking all doors and encasing the perimeter with high fences is supposed to thwart the shooter. Some entities go so far as to publicize the event with a story in the local news. One school district retrofit all the classrooms' exterior doors with different locking mechanisms that will allow teachers to lock the door from inside the classroom, instead of from the outside. The local news not only reported the new locks but also revealed that the school district has spent or will spend over $2 million on this change.

Although locks are a great start, this defense strategy still falls short. The lock only addresses limited physical security and does nothing to address the personal safety of any individual within the facility. Internally based shooters already have access to the school or facility and (as has been repeatedly demonstrated) have still managed to bring their weapons with them regardless. It should also be noted that in the design of some older elementary schools, classrooms are linked in a cluster. Once an event begins in one classroom, that person will have unhindered access to at least ten other classrooms within that same wing. Therefore, exterior door locks alone will not completely stop the shooter. For these reasons, faculty and staff still need to know how to address their own personal safety needs, and those of their students, by learning to properly shelter and hide and shelter to fight if the shooter should breach their location.

Check the Box

Condensed training on the subject is provided by some entities who subscribe to the quick and easy version of training. The participants are given a very simplistic answer to a very complex problem. This quick and easy fix works to "check the box" by being able to document that training has been done. One employee of a cable television provider stated that their training was done online, where employees simply watched a short video on the subject. This simple action was all the training they received on the subject.

Be careful of misinterpreting "training in emergency operations" as "training for your survival." In speaking with one school district, I learned that their focus was on complying with FEMA (Federal Emergency Management Association) and ensuring that all their people obtained their FEMA certifications in incident command systems (ICS). While the structure of the response to a critical incident is very important, it is largely for people who are first responders and is of minimal help to the people already caught up in the attack.

Hide and Hope Method

Some agencies have invested a little more time in the topic and have worked with local news media to provide video solutions for adults. This training recommends potential victims to hide in a place out of the shooter's view and hope they will not be discovered by the shooter. The video depicted victims hiding inside cabinets, closets, and other areas, where they wait to be rescued by law enforcement. Teaching and advocating that adults, who may be capable of fighting for their lives, give up any possibility of effective resistance and instead resort to hiding in this fashion places the shooter in total control over the lives of all potential victims in those hiding places should their shooter/ assailant locate them.

One example of how this strategy does not work can be seen in a shooting on July 1, 2009 at a dental office in Simi Valley, California. The husband of an employee showed up at his wife's place of work and shot and killed his estranged wife. Several female employees of the dental practice hid inside a closet. The shooter located the females hiding inside the closet and shot these women with his AK-47. To verify that the hide-and-hope strategy is not tactically sufficient, simply ask any off-duty law enforcement officer what they would do in a similar situation. Would that off-duty and unarmed officer run into a room, hide in a closet, and wait for authorities to hopefully arrive in the nick of time? Unlikely. Instead, the off-duty law enforcement officer would opt for the "shelter and fight" alternative. The officer would assume the worst case scenario, prepare for the encounter, and be physically and psychologically ready to fight for their life. The off-duty officer would consider the possibility of the shooter entering that area and would have a surprise party to **meet, greet, and defeat** the shooter, either with an improvised weapon taken from the current environment or with bare hands.

One might say that not everyone can be a highly trained law enforcement officer and therefore know what to do in order to defeat an active shooter/assailant. However, with knowledge and directed training on this subject, the reader can be every bit as good as a highly trained, unarmed, off-duty officer in a similar situation.

Keeping the Status Quo

Shooters have demonstrated that they will use a variety of methods to perpetrate their attacks, and these seem to evolve with almost each shooting incident. In order to be capable of mitigating the bizarre imagination of the assailant, training for citizens should also evolve to be current with the level and demonstrated sophistication of the shooter. Instead, organizations and their trainers fail to keep current with common tactics. This failure allows the next shooter to unleash unprecedented carnage and pandemonium on unsuspecting victims.

The very people who are supposed to provide and develop training have a limited scope of tactics. The shooters will only be bounded by their imagination and their knowledge of previous shooting events. Trainers appear to apply "in the box" solutions against an assailant who will likely bring "out of the box" attacks. An organization's inability to use trending active shooter/assailant information in their training, coupled with their limited imagination, can result in a population that is left virtually defenseless. Trainers should not use the same old tactics, which have been proven countless times to not be effective. What is needed is a multi-faceted approach where the defensive postures, tactics, and techniques take into account the potential shooter's imagination and the defenders use their creativity while crafting defensive strategies. When it comes to shooting events, leaders should consider and apply a full range of mitigation efforts in order to save lives.

The response strategies sanctioned by school officials and practiced by students around the nation provide an excellent example of this phenomenon. In 1951, students were taught to take shelter under a desk in the event of a nuclear attack. In more recent times, students are taught to take shelter under a desk in the event of an earthquake. Today, students are still taught to take shelter beneath a desk in the event of an active shooting. This same response has been used to shelter our school children since at least 1951. It is time for a change in response tactics. I will not advocate that students of any level be the ones to take on the active shooter/assailant. However, the person who is responsible for their safety should be provided with reasonable alternatives to adequately protect the students from an active threat.

Ignorance and arrogance combine to create a recipe for disaster. I have found a variety of organizations, including schools, hospitals, and private businesses, that have done nothing new to address such threats since their initial training. When reviewing several hospitals' policies on shooting threats, I noticed that some facilities only have a one-page document that comprises everything they will disclose to their personnel on the threat. Their training on the subject is just as brief. Many administrators act as if this threat is so rare that it does not exist. They act as if by providing additional information, they might be inviting the event to occur at their facility.

In an attempt to offer training for one major company, I provided them with a DVD that highlighted all aspects of training and defensive strategies that could be used to protect against an active shooter. After approximately one month of negotiations, the company finally announced that they did not have the finances for training for that year. When asked about returning the promotional DVD, they advised me that their Human Resource/Risk Manager had discarded it. When provided with an actual, tangible item that could save lives, they threw it in the trash.

It has also been my experience that some management officials prefer to employ the "don't rock the boat" response to any threat. The more they feel threatened, the softer they sit inside the boat. Because they do not want anything to happen, these leaders will do anything to prevent new information from entering their organizations. Not only will they do nothing to help mitigate the threat, but they will also actively prevent anyone else from coming to help.

At one southern California school district, their Administrative Risk Management section stated that they were embracing the ICS (Incident Command System) and that each of their personnel would receive their ICS certification. I tactfully explained that ICS does not provide victims of a shooting event with any tactics or techniques to save their lives. This manager refused to hear any details, however brief. This manager could not be persuaded to watch a ten-minute DVD that highlighted possible training on this subject.

Scare Tactics Approach

In February 2014, a training session for employees at a mall in a major southern California city was provided by the local police department. During this training session, police showed numerous slides depicting case studies of shooting events that had occurred across the country. For almost the entire ninety-minute presentation, police bombarded the attendees with slides illustrating the graphic carnage inflicted during past shootings. This only served to frighten the audience rather than provide any realistic advice or education. The flyer for the training was entitled "Active Shooter Procedures" and said that victims should lock their gates, hide in the back, run, hide, and fight. Very little time was spent discussing how individuals could fight back or otherwise ensure their safety during a shooting. Potential victims deserve and need much more than simple instructions to run, hide, and hope that the police arrive soon.

Relying on Their Reputation Methodology

The choice of training provider should not be based solely on who is providing the training, but should instead be based on the quality of the information. Governmental agencies have authored pamphlets that provide citizens with information on how to respond to an active shooter, but fall short on common sense tactics.

Agencies even mandated that, in the event of a shooting incident, employees should be trained to escape to a pre-arranged rally point. This is problematic advice because if the shooter is an employee or former employee, the pre-arranged rally point is compromised and the shooter will know exactly where to go to continue their rampage.

During earlier iterations of their training, the agency advocated making oneself large and yelling loudly in order to discourage the shooter. While this advice may work for scaring away wildlife, it may further enrage the shooter. Using that tactic likely only serves to make the individual a bigger target for the shooter. It was also advised to throw office supplies and furniture at the shooter as a distraction. Throwing a stapler or a chair is never a viable way to protect yourself from bullets fired from any firearm and will never equal the lethal capacity of an armed assailant in possession of an AK-47 assault rifle, a shotgun, or a semi-automatic handgun.

DVDs have also been produced that provide a variety of response strategies, but these are often not tactically sound. One of the first depicts a conference room where a meeting is apparently taking place. There are at least eight adults present at a long conference table. When the shooting starts, each adult ducks underneath the table to hide from that shooter. This strategy is called **Hide and Hope** and is for people who are unwilling or unable to fight for their lives. When several people are hiding under a huge conference table, they no longer have the mobility to do anything and are completely at the mercy of the shooter. The Columbine shooters demonstrated this principle when they coldly shot people hiding underneath a table.

Rather than merely telling people to hide under tables, provide them with usable options, tactics, and techniques that have a realistic chance of saving their lives. For example, the video depicts people escaping from the building via a glass door. One person stops immediately outside, retrieves a cell phone, and begins to call 911. This person is still within the kill zone and should move far away from the building before making any calls. The video also discusses warning others not to enter the building and shows an individual about to enter the building when someone else runs up and physically grabs them, explaining the danger and advising them to stay away. When you notice others approaching the danger zone, use your voice to warn them. Never leave a place of safety to run back to the building where the shooter is located.

In a different online training video, a former member of a highly recognized military unit advocated his version of techniques and tactics that could potentially place people in further harm. While his techniques do seek to engage the shooter, they often leave the weapon in the hands of the shooter after several initial movements have been made. Other techniques he performed had too many steps required to disarm the shooter, which allows them to continue firing. One of his tactics actually dislodges the weapon, but sends the shooter's handgun flying away from the shooter. This is problematic, as whenever an assailant is disarmed, the weapon needs to be in the hands of the defender, who will need a functioning weapon if/when the shooter reaches for a secondary weapon. After the initial confrontation, the defender should always be able to use that weapon against the shooter if necessary.

In their quest to provide information, tactics, and techniques to the general population, many who lack real firsthand tactical expertise have relied on the reputation of their unit, organization, or former occupation. We have seen that shooters are not concerned with a person's reputation or occupation. If given the opportunity, they will shoot anyone and everyone in their path, regardless of that person's qualifications.

Two supposed experts in their field conducted an active shooter webinar where a number of participants appeared to be more concerned about receiving the continuing education credit for the training rather than the actual content. After satisfying the participants that they would receive credit, the leaders encouraged their audience to adopt the Run, Hide, and Fight concept (advocated by a United States government agency) and suggested that people do the following, if they have to fight:

1. Attack until the shooter no longer represents a threat.
2. Throw objects at the shooter.
3. Shout and scream loudly during the attack.
4. Fight for your life.

Of the four tactics proposed for potential victims to use when faced with an active shooter, only 50 percent are accurate. For a potential victim to throw objects at the shooter while shouting and screaming loudly during the attack simply draws attention to the potential victim and makes them the next obvious target. This webinar advocates attacking the shooter as a last resort.

Specific instructions on how to launch an effective counterattack against an armed assailant are consistently absent from this webinar and from many other trainings used by a variety of organizations. The tactics that are advocated are ineffective against a person armed with a lethal weapon. Using ineffective fighting movements, such as kicking, kneeing, elbowing, or punching, should not be a part of active shooter training. Movements of that nature take a significant period of time (usually years) to achieve competence, and performing them without proper training can cause serious injuries to the defender and may not have the intended effect on the assailant.

Be wary of people who only use their current or former occupation as a source of credibility. Don't believe everything that you see or hear. Take the time to investigate matters that pertain to the protection of your life, your coworkers' lives, and the lives of your family.

How to Evaluate Active Shooter/Assailant Defense Training

How can a person, either individually or on behalf of an organization, evaluate the trainers who present active shooter training and chose the best one? Use the following criteria to evaluate potential active shooter trainers who could provide "realistic" training:

- What are the qualifications and experience of the person(s) providing the training?
- Where did the person obtain those qualifications and expertise?
- Does the method use a multi-faceted approach to providing solutions?
- Do they recommend the same old pool of limited solutions?

- Is the person well versed in all areas of the recommended active shooter strategies/solutions?
- Are the tactics, strategies, and solutions reasonable?
- Would that trainer use those same tactics and techniques, and advocate for their loved ones to use them, to defend against an active shooter?
- Are physical techniques taught in the fight portion of the training?
- Are the physical techniques realistic and effective?
- Does the physical technique expeditiously disarm and incapacitate the assailant, whether the assailant is armed with a handgun, long gun, or edged weapon?
- Do the techniques used to disarm an assailant allow the defender to incapacitate the assailant using no more than three moves?
- If the threat were a dangerous animal (as an example, a tiger) does the training teach tactics and techniques that would allow the defenders to adequately defend themselves, or does it merely instruct the defenders to hide and wait for authorities to respond to neutralize the threat?

Today's active shooters/assailants are mostly armed with guns and/or knives. Knowledge of how to successfully defend against any of these armed assailants (the "fight" portion of Run, Hide, and Fight) is of vital importance! Innocent citizens deserve the ability to be provided realistic, practical, easy, and effective lifesaving tactics and techniques against those who threaten their lives. All physical techniques should be capable of getting the primary weapon out of the shooter's hands in a minimal amount of movements and placing it in the hands of the defender, who will then have the opportunity to use the appropriate level of force to stop any further aggression from the armed assailant.

Part 3
Prevention and Early Detection

··

Preventing an active shooter is, at best, a partial solution. The acts of a person engaged in a killing episode are usually unpredictable as to where and when they will occur. Take into account that the shooter/assailant has chosen the date, the time, and the location for the event and will bring all the items needed to start their deadly rampage. When there are significant clues present and the appropriate actions are taken to stop the event from occurring, the event might just be prevented. The best chance of preventing a shooting rests on being proactive and employing public and/or private threat management principles to recognize a person who may be a threat. It is then necessary to use a variety of methods to intervene and make the environment safer for everyone.

A number of school shooting cases refer to the shooter being bullied. *Bully proofing* a child or youth can be done, but it will take significant effort and time and should begin prior to the child attending school. Getting your child involved in activities that boost self-esteem is vital to their self-confidence. A person with self-confidence can psychologically mitigate the effects of bullying. Teaching your child to physically protect themselves has several positive outcomes: it can help to keep your child's self-esteem high, and should physical bullying take place, your child is physically capable of defending themselves.

Some schools make it a policy to punish both the physical aggressor and the child who is attempting to protect themselves against an unwanted and unprovoked physical attack. If your school or school district has a policy such as this, that policy is unrealistic and not congruent with any municipal law. Nearly every city allows a person the right to self-defense in the event of a physical attack, and schools should be no different. This nonsensical policy was in effect when my children were attending public school. I told my children never to start a fight. I also told them that if they were attacked, they should defend themselves. I added that if their school disciplined them for merely defending themselves, I would reward their self-defense efforts by spending the day with them and declaring that day as their day. I am happy to report that day never occurred.

Noticing Pre-Incident Behaviors

Pre-incident behaviors are behaviors exhibited by shooters/assailants prior to the event. These behaviors can lead others to believe that this person or persons may commit mass murder. Authorities and organizational leaders should use caution in responding to these behaviors. If a person or persons have exhibited some of these indicators, steps should be taken to fully investigate all of the relevant issues surrounding the person(s) involved. This does not mean that an individual displaying these behaviors will be the next shooter, only that competent intervention should occur immediately to prevent any potential event.

On June 30, 2015, CNN reported that the neighbors of the shooters and homicide bombers from the Istanbul attack noticed the anti-social nature of these suspects. The neighbors noted that these suspects never opened their window coverings, but did open their windows for ventilation. Neighbors then noticed a strong odor of chemicals.

Family members, friends, coworkers, and neighbors can and should note these pre-incident behaviors and act on them before they escalate. Be sure to note any change in their "normal" behavior patterns and whether this person is exhibiting many of these behaviors, rather than just a few.

The following behaviors can be noticed by coworkers, supervisors, managers, or others that indicate warning signs that could lead to a violent episode:

- Crying, sulking, or temper tantrums
- Excessive absenteeism or lateness
- Disregard for the health and safety of others
- Disrespect for authority
- Increased mistakes, errors, or unsatisfactory work quality
- Refusal to acknowledge job performance problems
- Faulty decision making
- Testing the limits to see what they can get away with
- Swearing or emotional language
- Overreacting to criticism
- Making inappropriate statements
- Forgetfulness, confusion, or distraction
- Inability to focus
- Blaming others for mistakes
- Complaints of unfair treatment
- Talking about the same problems repeatedly without resolving them
- Insistence that they are always right
- Misinterpretation of communication from supervisors or coworkers
- Social isolation
- Poor or ignored personal hygiene
- Sudden and/or unpredictable change in energy level
- Complaints of unusual and/or non-specific illnesses

History of Violence

- Fascination with weapons or acts of violence
- Demonstrated violence toward inanimate objects
- Evidence of earlier violent behavior

Threatening Behavior

- Stating an intention to hurt someone (verbal or written)
- Holding grudges
- Excessive and inappropriate behavior (e.g. phone calls, gift-giving, stalking)
- Escalating threats that appear well-planned
- Preoccupation with violence

Intimidating Behavior

- Being argumentative
- Displaying unwarranted anger
- Being uncooperative, impulsive, easily frustrated
- Challenging peers and authority figures

Increase in Personal Stress

- An unreciprocated romantic obsession
- Serious family or financial problems
- Recent job loss

Negative Personality Characteristics

- Being suspicious of others
- Believing they are entitled to something
- Being unable to take criticism
- Feeling victimized

- Showing a lack of concern for the safety or well-being of others
- Low self-esteem

Marked Changes in Mood or Behavior

- Extreme or bizarre behavior
- Irrational beliefs and ideas
- Appearing depressed or expressing hopelessness or heightened anxiety
- Marked decline in work performance

Socially Isolated

- History of negative interpersonal relationships
- Few family or friends
- Seeing the company as a replacement family
- Having an obsessive involvement with their job

Public threat management principles are a set of previously identified policies and procedures that are used in the workplace. Each worksite that employs more than five employees could benefit from robust threat policies. Those items will be elaborated later. It should be mandatory that a written policy be created that identifies threatening behavior (verbal and nonverbal) in the workplace. The policy should articulate when threatening behavior is observed as well as what steps will be taken to identify, address, and ultimately resolve the threat. The policy needs to address the needs of the potential victim(s), the organization, and the offending person. This policy needs to be followed explicitly.

Private threat management principles are those that can be used by people outside of the workplace, in relation to their family, friends, and neighbors. These principles identify threatening behavior and actions by the suspected individual that reasonably lead others to believe that the person is heading toward a violent episode. As an example, a person may have communicated plans to hurt others by using a social media site or by mentioning them (sometimes as a passing or insignificant comment) to friends or family members. In those plans, the person may have indicated the place where the event will occur, or most likely, the intended targets.

In one case, a school shooter told his friends to bring their cameras to school the following day and to not be in a certain area. That area was the intended location of the shooting. When anyone becomes aware that someone is in the process of gathering weapons, or is making plans, or even mentions an intent to take violent actions against others, that person has a duty as a compassionate and caring individual to do everything possible to stop that violent act from occurring.

People can and should report their observations of pre-incident behaviors to the appropriate sources to protect innocent lives. Taking those proactive steps to thwart the actions of the potential shooter may involve notification of law enforcement so that they may intervene prior to the deadly encounter. If a person has been identified as a potential threat to others, law enforcement agencies need to partner with the person's family and mental health professionals to ensure the protection of all concerned.

Psychological intervention alone may stop the potential shooter. Most, if not all, jurisdictions provide an avenue by which threatening individuals can be seen by a physician to determine if they are a threat to themselves or others. If a person is deemed a threat, hopefully the healing process can begin. Observation or intervention by mental health professionals at an appropriate facility may be just what the potential shooter needs to stop them from resorting to deadly violent behavior. This is where the system can and has fallen apart. When others note the pre-incident behavioral indicators and chose to either ignore the situation or take minimal steps to defuse it, the act can go on as planned by the assailant.

On May 24, 2014, in Isla Vista, California (Santa Barbara County), a suspect moved to ten different locations, where he stabbed, shot, and used his vehicle to kill six victims before he was engaged by law enforcement. The suspect ultimately took his own life during that confrontation. Law enforcement officers found three semi-automatic handguns with 400 unspent rounds in the suspect's vehicle. All of these items were legally purchased. There had been warning signs the suspect was struggling with his mental health. His mother came across his YouTube videos one month earlier after she had not heard from him. She called his therapist, who then called a Santa Barbara mental health care hotline.

The video shows the suspect sitting in a car and looking at a camera, laughing often, and saying that he is going to take revenge against humanity. He describes loneliness and frustration because girls have never been attracted to him and says that, at age twenty-two, he is still a virgin. The video, which is almost seven minutes long, appears scripted. The suspect states that he would take great pleasure in slaughtering all of them, as they would finally see that he is truly the superior alpha male. The woman on the hotline called police to check on him.

Six policemen arrived at the suspect's residence in Isla Vista on April 30, but they found nothing alarming. The officers told the suspect to call his mother and reassure her that he was okay. The Santa Barbara County sheriff stated that at the time, the deputies determined that the subject did not meet the criteria for an involuntary mental health hold. In hindsight, the suspect's parents now feel that the welfare check by police was a pivotal moment and a missed opportunity to really find out what was going on with their son.

The suspect also left behind a 107,000-word document detailing what he called his "twisted world." He e-mailed this to his parents and a therapist the day he went on his killing rampage, and it was ultimately located by investigators and journalists as well. The central theme of "My Twisted World" is his virginity, which he blamed on the "cruelness" of women. The suspect himself wrote in his manifesto that he worried that someone had discovered his plan when the police visited. He feared that police would demand to search his room and would therefore discover all the weapons he had amassed and his written plans, leading to his imprisonment and denial of his planned "revenge." The suspect suffered from undisclosed mental health issues and was under the care of a variety of care professionals. He had been seeing therapists on and off since he was eight years old. When the suspect attended high school, he met with a therapist almost every day. Before his death, the suspect was seeing two therapists. The suspect passed the background check needed to purchase the firearms used in the shooting, and nothing had been found in the investigation to indicate that he should have been disqualified. There were so many missed opportunities where the assailant possibly could have been treated and/or government agencies could have intervened with their full resources to thwart the crimes, but due to inadequate policies and practices, the deadly event occurred.

In November of 2016, a man who had been deployed to Iraq and subsequently discharged appeared at the Anchorage, Alaska office of the F.B.I. and advised that he believed that the Islamic State (a terrorist organization) was attempted to control his mind, forcing him to watch ISIS propaganda videos. The man was transferred to the custody of local law enforcement who submitted the man to local mental health care professionals for psychological evaluation. On January 6, 2017, that same man arrived on a commercial flight to the Ft. Lauderdale International Airport and retrieved his checked bag from the baggage claim area. The man entered the restroom, retrieved his handgun from his checked luggage, loaded the firearm and exited the restroom where he shot eleven people, killing five. The man surrendered to police once confronted. During news coverage on the day the shooting occurred, the man's brother advised the news media that the shooter had experienced mental problems. The question will be asked for some time whether or not the shooter's brother, other family members or his significant other had more of a responsibility to ensure the shooter did not have access to a firearm and possibly could have prevented this shooting.

When a person is diagnosed with a "serious and significant" psychological condition <u>where they could be a threat to themselves or others</u>, any and all firearms need to be removed from the person's possession. Great care should also be taken to ensure that they have no available means to obtain a firearm or other deadly weapon for the foreseeable future. When issues arise to impact the safety of the public, lawmakers, together with other stakeholders, can come together to craft a better system to protect the public from someone who has been deemed a threat. The family members of the affected person need to take a proactive role through diligent observation as well as following through with preventative actions to ensure their family member is not in possession of dangerous weapons. If the family member has weapon(s) on their property, significant care needs to be used to ensure the affected person has no means of obtaining that weapon. If the weapon cannot be secured with 100 percent certainty, the weapon(s) should be relinquished to someone who can adequately secure those weapons.

In the Carson City, Nevada, International House of Pancakes case, the shooter had a significant history of mental illness and regular access to numerous firearms. His family was well aware of his mental illness and the fact that he had numerous firearms, yet they chose to not take any action and allowed the shooter to keep his firearms. Perhaps they believed it would never become an issue. In 2014, Nevada was considering legislation whereby family members of a person whose mental wellbeing is at risk may seek a restraining order for authorities to retrieve and maintain the firearms for public safety.

Law enforcement may also utilize the criminal justice system to take legal action by confiscating illegal and dangerous weapons and taking individuals into custody for the violation of criminal laws. When those individuals pose a clear and present danger to any section of the community, law enforcement has shown that they can act proactively, particularly when the potential shooter has indicated specific individuals on a hit list of potential targets. While our society allows for its citizens to possess arms in some jurisdictions, it may allow authorities to remove those arms if they reasonably believe that the potential shooter has a firearm and has begun the steps to commit mass murder. Succinctly reiterated, any person with a significant history of acute mental illness who could pose a danger to themselves or others should not have access to one or more firearms.

Awareness and Observation Skill

When you are in any public place, you need to have all of your senses working. In this technological age, many people lack situational awareness and are oblivious to the actions of others. People can be so engrossed in their electronic devices that they tune out their visual, auditory, and physical surroundings. Those that do so are at risk of missing vital danger signals that may otherwise provide them with clues that something is tragically wrong.

In many cases, the shooter approached and entered the location with a gun already in hand. Whenever you see a firearm in an unusual context, assume that your safety is at risk. Take immediate evasive action and contact law enforcement to report what you have just noticed.

In the current climate, when active shootings are more common, anyone who legally possesses a firearm and carries it into an area where such weapons are not common may be subjected to closer scrutiny by law enforcement. Even law-abiding and legally armed citizens may be confronted by law enforcement and asked to justify why they are armed in that particular area. While I would not advocate breaking the law, if you are legally armed, take whatever actions that you feel you can justify (in a criminal and civil court) to save your life—including intervening in an active shooting or carrying your legal firearm with you into different locations. I strongly encourage each person to know the laws in your state concerning the justification and use of deadly force and to stay within the elements of those laws.

Signs that an active shooter is present include shots fired, people screaming, wounded or dead individuals, and individuals taking cover. Additionally, you may actually see an individual (or group of individuals) moving through an area carrying a firearm and shooting at people.

Two philosophies that govern my personal safety are these: first, it is better to have and to not need than to need and not have, and second, I would much rather be judged by twelve (peers in a jury) than carried by six (in a coffin).

The development of observational skills is vital for your survival. When going about your daily routine, develop a sense of situational awareness where you are cognizant of your environment. This is when you see or hear something that seems wrong, or when you feel uncomfortable due to the absence of something indescribable that should be present. Police call this feeling JDLR (just does not look right). You need to notice the danger signs. When you observe people in any environment who are armed, immediately consider the context and determine if you need to take action to save your own life or the lives of those around you.

Whenever you enter a new environment, conduct a visual scan of all people within that immediate area with the single purpose of evaluating whether they pose a threat to your physical safety. Making that safety scan allows you to determine whether you will remain or quickly exit a location. You will be looking for people whose demeanor, behavior, manner of dress, and objects in their possession are alarming or threatening.

For example, passengers noticed a man behaving strangely on a train and summoned police. However, before police could arrive, the man produced a knife and stabbed several people. When the police finally arrived, the knife-wielding subject was subdued and taken into custody. In this case, the man's strange behavior gave away his malicious intentions before the deadly acts began.

Wearing unusual or suspicious clothing, especially a ballistic vest, is a sign that an individual may have violent intentions. Currently there are only two groups of people who would or could wear ballistic vests and related material while engaging in the lawful performance of their duties: law enforcement and military personnel. Any other person or group should be viewed as a threat to public safety. In the case of the Colorado movie theater shooting, the suspect was wearing ballistic armor and a gas mask during the shooting. If a person had spotted the suspect wearing that type of attire prior to the shooting, lives might have been saved.

If a person is carrying a bag, backpack, duffle bag, or any other unusual case, this could reflect violent intentions. In several cases, the suspects concealed their weapons and additional ammunition inside such cases when they entered the location. The shooting inside a McDonald's restaurant in San Ysidro, California, in 1984 had this type of weapon concealment.

In several shootings, the shooter was observed entering the building carrying a long gun. In the modern era, there is no reason for an individual to enter any public place with such a weapon. Recognition of the overt presence of such a weapon should result in immediate action.

Once you have completed a visual scan of your environment and deemed it safe, this does not mean that it will remain so. This does not mean that you should be on the constant lookout for bad people. However, in order to maintain a comfortable level of safety for you and your loved ones, it is always a good idea to do a periodic check of your environment. When new people enter and exit your environment, place them under the same scrutiny that you originally placed everyone else under. There have been shooting incidents where the shooters first entered the environment to ensure they could conduct their horrific crimes, only to leave and return moments later to begin their rampage. Watching people as they approach and exit your area will allow you to better see danger signs.

Physical Characteristics of a Covertly/Overtly Armed Person

Having the ability to spot individuals who may be covertly or overtly armed with a handgun is a skill that, with diligent practice, can become part of a person's situational awareness.

In cities or counties where it is legal to open-carry (i.e. openly carry a handgun, usually in a holster), the weapon will typically be worn where it can be easily retrieved using the person's dominant hand, such as in their waistband.

For people who covertly carry a handgun (legally and illegally), they will also conceal their weapons where they are easily accessible with their dominant hand. For almost 90 percent of the population, this is the right hand.

Some of the most common locations to conceal a handgun are these:

- On the waistband between the stomach and hip on the dominant side
- In a jacket or pants pocket on the dominant side
- In an ankle holster inside the left ankle or on the outside of the right ankle.
- Beneath the left arm and armpit, fastened to the waist.

The outline of the weapon (or at least a slight bulge) may be noticeable under the person's clothing. For a large-caliber handgun, the weapon will have a significantly larger bulge. The weapon may also be revealed through creases or stretch lines in a tight-fitting garment, such as a shirt or sweater. Depending on how the weapon was concealed in the waistband, the barrel or grip of the handgun may be visible while the rest of the weapon is concealed.

The person who is carrying a concealed handgun will also exhibit some of the following behaviors, although these do not reflect whether they are legally concealing a weapon or not:

- When the armed person has completed, or is in the process of completing, a moderate to gross physical movement (getting up from a seated position, putting on or taking off a jacket), the person will be seen touching or manipulating firearm to secure it in place. This is particularly visible when the armed person is standing up, as they will make security adjustments with the hand, wrist, or forearm on the side where the handgun is concealed.
- When the armed person is in a crowd, they hold one arm closer to their body to support the gun and to ensure that it is not jostled out of place.
- When the person is running or walking fast, they will tend to hold the firearm firmly with a hand or wrist, or press it against their body, to prevent the weapon from moving.

- People who are illegally concealing a firearm, if confronted by authority figures, will tend to turn their armed side away from the person confronting them.

Keep in mind that not all legally armed persons will have a clean-cut appearance. In fact, some undercover police officers need to have their physical appearance model that of a very unsavory character. Never ask if someone is "on the job" or "undercover." If you are in doubt, leave the area and contact your local law enforcement agency to report the person and the conduct you observed. Allow the police to do their jobs by locating the individual, deciding if any laws have been broken, and taking the appropriate actions to ensure everyone's safety.

Survivor Mindset

There are many things you can do to ensure your safety before and during an active shooting. Always be alert and aware of your environment whenever you are outside of your home. This will help ensure your safety and the safety of others around you.

Prepare yourself in advance for the potential of a deadly encounter. Following the deadly terrorist attack that occurred in Mumbai, India, on November 26, 2008, it became apparent how prepared the terrorists were. They struck at several locations throughout the city, killing at least 164 people (both civilians and security personnel). Nine attackers were killed during the counterassault by elite troops. The terrorists had planned for months (if not years) in advance and appear to have executed their plan efficiently and without significant difficulty. However, when authorities were forced to respond, police and military personnel were overwhelmed.

Many organizations and people think that such a horrific event could never happen. Since no attack of this type has ever happened, they do not feel that they need to prepare. In these situations, the occurrence of many deadly shootings across the country provides the larger population with one advantage, as they provide us with vital information about how shooters often plan their premeditated events for long periods of time before executing them. This should provide us with the motivation to begin planning our own survival strategies: mentally, physically, financially, and spiritually.

Mental Preparation

Be a people watcher. The bad guys won't always look like bad guys or wear "bad guy" clothes. However, you do want to pay attention to people's clothing, demeanor, and behavior. Be aware of how a person is dressed and whether this is appropriate for the environment, the season, or the event. Watch their demeanor. Are their characteristics consistent with their environment? Do they appear overly inattentive to environmental stimulus? Are they perhaps focused on something completely different from the people around them?

Listen for the sounds of shots fired. Witnesses of active shootings report that they heard booms or pops, depending on the size (caliber) of the firearm used. The sounds associated with shots fired will depend on several factors. These include the type of weapon used, the distance the shooter is from your location, and the acoustics of the location where the shots were fired. Listen for the sounds of people running and raised or screaming voices. You may also hear items being destroyed as people attempt to escape or as bullets hit them. If you are outside, the sounds of multiple sirens approaching your location could alert you that something has gone wrong, even if you are unable to hear the initial shots fired. Multiple police personnel arriving on a scene and the presence of heavily armed SWAT personnel should also signal that a deadly incident is occurring. When you notice any of these danger signs appear, it is best to quickly move out of the way of arriving emergency personnel and allow them access to the area. You should take this opportunity to evacuate the immediate area.

Know and listen for the sound of a weapon is being reloaded or discarded. This sound may alert you to the perfect moment for you, and any of your fellow defenders, to launch a counterattack on the shooter. In several cases, the shooter either needed to reload a weapon or discard it to draw another. During the shooting rampage at Luby's Cafeteria, the shooter reloaded several times and still had ammunition remaining when law enforcement arrived and engaged the shooter, who ultimately killed himself. The shooting of US Representative Gabrielle Giffords at a political support rally occurred in the parking lot of a supermarket. The shooter approached Congresswoman Giffords and shot her in the head at point-blank range with a semi-automatic handgun. The shooter continued to shoot others present at the site. A total of six people were killed and eighteen others wounded. When the shooter attempted to reload his weapon, others in the crowd were able to subdue him.

If you are present during an active shooting, be aware of the shooter's actions and take full advantage of any moment in which the shooter is not firing, either due to reloading a weapon, discarding a weapon, or a weapon's malfunction.

Know your escape routes. Always know at least two different routes you can use during an emergency. If you are very familiar with an area (a workplace or school), locate the escape routes you could use during an emergency in advance of any event. Ensure that the doors you would use can in fact be opened and are not locked with a key. Many businesses are required by fire department regulations to have specific doors unlocked during the hours they are open for business. If you are unsure as to whether the doors would be locked or unlocked, you could ask the management. Certain doors have an audible alarm that is activated once the door is opened. Rather than open doors yourself and activate the alarm, you could ask the management.

Determine where an exit door leads. You want as much information as possible to avoid being disoriented during an actual emergency. For example, a mall will have several doors that are used by the store employees, delivery people, or maintenance. You may not be permitted to use those doors, but you do want to know if the doorway leads to a hallway with no exit, or if the doors lead to an exit to the outside.

Make mental notes of your environment, especially in public. Sit in places facing the door to facilitate your ability to see people as they are entering the area. Notice people within that environment, specifically their clothing styles, bags they may be carrying, or the obvious presence of firearms. In several cases, the suspect entered the location without attempting to conceal the firearm.

Remember that plainclothes or undercover law enforcement will be armed and may not be obviously members of the police. However, those individuals are usually very adept at concealing their firearms on their person and identifying themselves if they need to. If you unsure whether an individual carrying a weapon is doing so legally, you can always leave the area and call 911 to have that person checked by law enforcement. It is not your job to ask that person, have management ask that person, or wait around to learn the results of your curiosity.

Because criminals mix among the innocent civilian population, law enforcement officers (both uniformed and plainclothes detectives) may be involved with these criminals within the public domain. This can be in a number of capacities, such as surveillance or arresting an individual. Keep in mind that some undercover police officers are so convincing that they may not look like the stereotypical undercover cop. In fact, the officer may look more like a bad guy than a good guy. You may not be able to differentiate the good guy from the bad guy.

Most police procedures require that officers select the time and place of an arrest in order to limit the public's exposure to potential shots fired. However, some criminals may force a violent confrontation within the public domain, knowing that police may hesitate due to the presence of civilians. This confrontation may require officers to draw their weapons.

If you notice a uniformed officer, plainclothes detective, or any individual holding a firearm, regardless of who is holding the weapon, take immediate steps to leave the affected area without drawing attention to yourself. As soon as you are safe, contact law enforcement. Your job is not to intervene unless you are requested to do so by law enforcement or it is necessary to save your life. Your sole job is to get yourself and your loved ones to a safe place. Once in a safe place, you may contact law enforcement to advise them of what has transpired.

In very rare circumstances, you may be the only individual able to save the life of an officer who has been incapacitated by a suspect. There are examples of police officers who have been confronted with overwhelming physical force when conducting a routine arrest or traffic stop. Sometime the officer has been completely incapacitated and could have died without the chance intervention of a civilian. When you go about your daily business, look out for the officers who might be in danger and do what you can (within your abilities) to assist that officer.

Your help may come in the form of calling 911 or using the officer's radio to summon additional police assistance. You should tell them that an officer needs help, along with your location and a brief description of what is occurring. Your call for help will bring additional officers and emergency medical assistance.

There is a huge danger in using a firearm to come to an officer's rescue. I cannot advise that you should, or that you should not. You are the only one capable of making that determination. Know that if/when additional officers arrive on scene, those additional officers may not know that you are trying to help, and they may see you as a threat. You also may encounter violent resistance from the suspect, or associates of the suspect (who may or may not be immediately visible). I personally would come to the aid of the officer, but this based upon many years as a law enforcement officer and extensive martial arts training.

Situational awareness. Criminal profiling in the case of criminal gangs is an important part of your situational awareness. Most of today's gang members will dress the part. Gang members rarely worry about their outward appearances or attempt to blend in with society. If you do notice obvious gang members, be aware that their mere presence may be a risk to you, as they can evoke a violent response from a rival gang in the area. In past cases, innocent individuals have been shot or killed after being caught in the crossfire between rival gangs. Therefore, the best course of action is to be capable of identifying these types of criminals and leaving before any violence occurs.

On April 27, 2002, a planned special event motorcycle rally took place in Laughlin, Nevada. A fight between two rival motorcycle gangs erupted into a shooting that left three people dead and dozens hurt. The patrons of the major casino had to take cover amidst the hail of bullets. On September 23, 2011, another planned special event motorcycle rally took place in Sparks, Nevada. The event, called "Street Vibrations," is an annual week-long event that has drawn tens of thousands of motorcycle enthusiasts to the Reno-Sparks area. That year, a shooting erupted between two different motorcycle gangs that left the head of the San Jose, California, chapter dead and two other members wounded.

Criminal profiling (not racial profiling), in terms of spotting people who look like a threat, is also a good observation skill. Be aware of clothing that suggests that a person is carrying a concealed firearm. Remain alert to people who are carrying backpacks or duffle bags into an area where they are not common. Not everyone who has a backpack or duffle bag is a person intent on shooting up the place, but until you know, it would be a good idea to keep an eye on them.

Combine your observations of their clothing, behavior, and any accessories to determine if they are a threat to your safety. Fashion may lead some people to dress in a style that seems unusual, so it is important to consider their dress along with other observations. Are these people acting suspicious or in a manner that may lead others to feel that they have something to hide? There are times when people appear to fit into the environment, but their behavior gives them away.

On September 16, 2013, an employee of the Navy Yard entered his work area carrying a disassembled sawed-off shotgun in a bag on his shoulder. Once the shooter entered the bathroom on the fourth floor, he assembled the shotgun, exited the bathroom, and began shooting. Video surveillance indicates that the shooter crept through hallways in search of victims prior to beginning his rampage.

Once the shooter ran out of ammunition for his shotgun, he killed an armed security officer and obtained that officer's semi-automatic handgun. Police responded to the scene and engaged the suspect in a prolonged gun battle before the suspect was neutralized. If someone had been able to observe the suspect's surreptitious behavior in surveillance footage prior to the shootings, perhaps the outcome would have been different.

Most special events, such as concerts or athletic events, since 9/11 have been screening patrons before they enter the facility. Security personnel or other employees set up tables at the entry location and look into bags, large containers, and coats, looking for objects that could be a threat to public safety. At almost all of these events, they have failed to detect my conceal handgun. Does that mean that their security system is severely lacking? Perhaps they decided that I don't look like a bad guy and hence deemed me not a threat. Security staff at these events are in need of training on observing illegally armed patrons rather than looking for unauthorized food or alcoholic beverages.

On April 15, 2013, the Boston Marathon had police personnel present to detect suspicious devices and individuals. Among the thousands of people present along the route, two individuals casually walked through the crowd and planted explosive devices hidden in backpacks near the finish line.

Seconds after the first bomb detonated, the second bomb exploded several hundred yards away. The blast killed three spectators and injured 264 other people. Although these domestic terrorists used bombs rather than firearms, it does suggest the need for greater scrutiny at large public events and the need to be even more vigilant.

Use your senses. Using your vision and hearing are two important methods of ensuring your safety. When you enter any environment, quickly scan the area for potentially dangerous people and to determine if the location appears normal. If you are seated inside, place yourself so that you can see others who enter the facility. This gives you a few extra seconds to react to any potential threat that enters through the front doors. If you spot danger and need to quickly escape, try to notify others of the threat. For example, you see a man entering a restaurant openly carrying a gun, and you believe that he is intending to commit a violent act. As you are escaping, it is usually safe to loudly yell "Gun!" Once you are safe, notify law enforcement. In the 2014 Wal-Mart shooting in Las Vegas, Nevada, one shopper saw the armed suspect enter the store and grabbed her belongings before escaping.

In the extreme event that you are wounded by gunfire, keep your wits about you. Being shot does not always mean that you will die. In some cases, individuals had sustained non – life threatening injuries, but convinced themselves there were going to die. The power of the mind is spectacular, and you should convince yourself that you will survive, no matter what. This type of mental rehearsal is an important technique and can be a major factor in your success or failure. When training for karate competitions, I would wear clothing that made me a champion, even though I had yet to attend the actual competition. I envisioned myself fighting my opponents, blocking their strikes, countering their movements with my own techniques, and scoring points to propel me to success.

I also needed to be in the right mental state (focused aggression—not anger) to properly execute the physical techniques. In my mind, I had already fought and won. It is important to state here that without the right mindset, the defender will lack the confidence to execute an attack at the right time. It will therefore be lacking and may prove unsuccessful.

Personal Survival Plan

- Locate two different ways to evacuate the area.
- Find two different locations where you could shelter and hide or shelter and fight.
- Locate items within your environment that could be used as improvised weapons if your armed assailant should breach your concealed hiding place.

- Learn, know, and continuously practice firearms disarming techniques. The ability to disarm a person who has a firearm is the most effective part of your survival plan should you have to fight.
- Know whom you can rely on should an emergency of this nature arise, whether a coworker, friend, or family member. You can coordinate with this person on what to do and in what order, should you need to shelter and fight. As an example, the first person to make contact with the shooter needs to focus on the primary weapon. The second person needs to focus on either the shooter's second weapon (should one be immediately visible) or on incapacitating the shooter by using a carotid hold
- Devise a code word for your family. There may be a time when you or your family members observe a threat that may not be apparent to everyone else. In such a case, a covert code word can be used to alert family members around you to the danger and how they should respond.

  Make sure to repeat the code words so that you are certain that your loved ones heard correctly. For example:
  - *Red 1:* There is a potential shooter. Everyone needs to follow me and quickly evacuate the area.
  - *Red 2:* There is a potential shooter. Everyone needs to follow me to a place where we can shelter and hide/fight.
- A designated family reunification plan. In the case that family members become separated in an emergency, the entire family needs to know where to go and how they will be reunited. Whenever you are in public with family members, select and share a location where you should meet in the case of an emergency. This communication should only take a few seconds, but they are well spent. You can also text your family members to advise them of your status, to arrange where you can all meet up, or to warn them of impending danger.

Physical Preparations

Any correctional officer who has guarded inmates in prison knows that they spend the majority of their time training, whether it is cardio, weights, or martial arts. In comparison, most of us work at our various jobs and then go home. Some of us drink a beer on the couch and watch TV to unwind. We eat unhealthy dinners, drink too much, stay up too late, and then do it all again the next day. Others do get the physical exercise we need, eat nutritious food, sleep enough, and are generally healthy. Which category are you in, and which category do you want to be in for your own survival? If you are among the former, now is a great time to start training and improving your health so you are in peak condition should you need for fight for survival.

Be sure to train for increased stamina as well as learning proper physical techniques. Stamina training is important for any prolonged physical exertions or short bursts of extreme activity. Aim to be strong enough to run a mile (non-stop), to sprint a couple of hundred yards, and to use your upper-body strength to propel yourself over obstacles. Additionally, knowing the most efficient and effective methods to incapacitate an assailant is key to your survival. You must know and regularly practice proper physical techniques so that you are capable of using them in a real altercation. You may need to use them all to escape or fight an active shooter.

Spiritual Preparation

Your spirituality and faith are the third part in preparing to survive an active shooting, as they will allow you to weather the shock and trauma of being involved in such a violent event. During an active shooting, the simple possibility of seeing deceased or severely injured people can be traumatic. Even soldiers and seasoned law enforcement officers who have seen this before can be severely impacted, so this is not a sign of weakness.

It is important to come to terms with the fact that you may need to use deadly force against another human being in order to protect your own life. Some people may have deeply-held religious reservations about taking another's life, even if it is to protect their own. You need to consider how you feel about this, and be firm in your decision so that you can act without hesitation should you find yourself present at an active shooting.

There is always the possibility that, despite a person's best survival efforts, they may be killed or seriously injured (physically or mentally). Coming to terms with your own mortality is something that never happens for most individuals until a deadly encounter is thrust upon them. During my time as a law enforcement officer, I had to come to terms with the idea that any day on the job could be last, since police officers can be killed during routine actions as well as when responding to violent incidents. It is important to always tell your family that you love them in case you never make it home. No one relishes the thought of considering their own death, but it was not my death that I feared while I was working as a police officer. Instead, it was the fear of suddenly and unexpectedly being taken away from my family. It was for that reason that I came to grips with my own mortality and felt somewhat at peace with my chosen calling.

You will not have the luxury of knowing the day and time of your last moment on this earth. Therefore, it is vitally important to resolve issues concerning your spirituality and embrace the people you care about and tell them how you truly feel often while you still have the chance. Always seek to keep your personal affairs in order to ensure your loved ones will not have any issues in obtaining items from your estate.

Sights, Sounds, and Defensive Reactions

When an individual has elected to go on a rampage, there is almost nothing that the average person can do other than to react to the threat. Perhaps the first indication that an active shooting is about to begin is when the shooter is observed just moments prior to the attack commencing.

The first few seconds of an active shooting can be the most critical. Upon hearing the sound of gunfire or observing an edged weapon attack, a common reaction can be the mistaken belief that the event is not real. Gunshots can be mistaken for fireworks, a car backfiring, or some commotion.

This misconception can delay the reactions of people, as they freeze in place instead of taking appropriate actions. The shooter uses this lag time as a way to attack even more victims. Once people do understand the acts are real, precious moments may have been lost. You may recognize that an active shooting is occurring in your vicinity either because the event is occurring in your immediate area or because you hear the gunshots or see the shooting from a distance. In either case, you want to be capable of distinguishing the "boom" sounds from a larger caliber firearm (a shotgun, rifle, or large caliber handgun) from the "pop" sounds from a smaller caliber weapon.

Other sights or sounds that you may be able to identify are those of people fleeing the area, attempting to flee, taking cover from the shooter, or wounded victims. If you see people fleeing from a location or hear the commotion of a hurried escape from any area, this is not the time to be inquisitive. It is also not the time to ignore them and go about your business as usual. Instead, keep their actions in mind and immediately leave the area. Perhaps they are reacting to a danger that you have not yet detected. Why enter the area and place yourself in danger if you don't need to?

Once you identify that shots have been fired, take immediate and appropriate actions to ensure your survival and the survival of others around you.

Adrenalin can have an impact upon how you react to an active shooting. Two physiological reactions that you might experience in a truly dangerous situation are auditory blocking and visual imparity.

When experiencing auditory blocking, a person may not be capable of hearing during the dangerous event. Visual imparity occurs when things begin to appear in slow motion. What occurs in these situations is that the brain is processing too many stimuli at once and so needs to close off certain functions (hearing) and slow down other functions (sight) in an attempt to process everything. These physiological symptoms can, and likely will, occur to those in an acutely dangerous situation. Once the situation is over, the brain returns to normal functioning. It is important to know that if these two reactions are present, you are most likely in danger, and you should react appropriately.

Notification of an Active Shooter Event

People can be advised of the presence of an active shooter by a variety of different means. The principal reasons for this notification are either to stop the event from occurring, to reduce the amount of bloodshed, or to speed up response by law enforcement to the active shooter.

Closed circuit television (CCTV) systems with recording capabilities are extremely valuable. The camera system should be set up so that coverage begins at the exterior of the facility's designated parking areas and extends into every major corridor within the building. Thus, visual information can be provided from the moment an individual is discovered at the exterior perimeter, and they can be monitored before they enter the building. Care should be taken to avoid blind spots, specifically in places where it is obvious to visitors that CCTV coverage is not provided.

Discovery of a threat prior to the event occurring is the best possible way to either stop a shooter or to reduce bloodshed. Therefore, the camera should be monitored in a secure control room. For entities that have more than one location (such as schools or other government buildings), the cameras should be accessible off-site as well. Cameras should be monitored by a person who is capable of identifying a potential threat and obtaining additional confirmation of the threat. As soon as a threat is detected on CCTV, the people within that environment should be notified, and specific contingency actions can be taken to mitigate the threat.

A *distinct audible alarm* should be employed and used to advise all within hearing range of the active shooter threat. The regular occupants of a building need to immediately recognize the audible alarm, and it should only be used for a real event. The alarm should be sounded once confirmation has been obtained that a shooter is either approaching the facility, is within the facility, or has begun a deadly rampage. Once the audible alarm is activated, occupants should take steps to ensure their safety, contingent upon the location of the shooter and the nature of the threat, if known.

This system could have been used during the January 6, 2017 shooting at the Ft. Lauderdale Airport. The shooter, who was a passenger on an incoming flight retrieved his gun from the baggage area, entered a restroom, loaded his weapon and exited the restroom firing at people within the baggage claim area. The shooter killed five people and shot another eight before surrendering to law enforcement. Although people within that immediate area reacted to the threat via the sound of gunfire, an audible alarm could have been activated to alert more people (passengers and airport employees) to the ongoing threat to facilitate safety.

A *public address system* was used in the 2014 Fort Hood shooting to warn others that the event was occurring. The disadvantage to using a public address system is that the person communicating the threat must speak in a clear and concise manner so that the listeners can fully understand the intended message. Problems can occur if the person delivering the message speaks too fast or indistinctly. The listeners must also listen without interruption to the entire message before responding to the threat, or there is potential for the incorrect response to occur. If this system is used alone, it can waste valuable time. Therefore, if this system is utilized at all, it should be preceded by the distinctive audible alarm.

Mass communication via text messages and electronic mail is a system that has been used to warn students on a college campus that an active shooter event is occurring. A designated person within that entity's administration must initiate the system. Recipients of the mass communication are warned to take specific actions to ensure their safety. Students and staff need to ensure that they are prepared to receive such critical text messages and e-mail alerts.

Part 4

Tactics and Techniques to Survive an Active Shooter/Assailant Event

··

When shots are fired, your immediate defensive actions will be contingent upon your current environment, such as the location of the shooter, the distance between you and the shooter, and any objects between you and the shooter. You will have at least three options: **escape** from the shooting location, **shelter to hide** inside the shooting environment, or **shelter to fight** within the shooting environment. All responses will be discussed.

When you recognize that shots have been fired, immediately crouch down and get as low to the ground as possible. Locate the direction where the shots are coming from and seek cover behind something that will protect you from bullets fired from that direction. A concrete wall, or a solid and heavy metal object would stop most bullets. If the object you have chosen as cover temporarily conceals you from the shooter, you should use that opportunity to look for a means of escape.

You may need to stay in that location until it is safe for you to move, which may only be after the shooting event is over. If you are able to escape the area, do not stop until you have placed another building between you and the last known location of the shooter. While you are in the process of escaping, it is your decision whether to help others to flee with you. If you can safely assist others to escape, please do. If you are unable to escape the area and are in immediate peril, stay close to the ground and shelter behind any available cover.

You may need to move to an area where you can shelter to hide. Remember to keep as quiet as possible. If you need to use your telephone, only do so once you are relatively safe. It is best to text, or otherwise silently notify, others about the situation.

They, in turn, can call the police and advise them of your situation and your location. Keep your cell phone fully charged as much as possible. You may think that you are just completing a quick errand, when in fact you may be there for several hours. Remember, only the shooter knows the place and time of the planned massacre.

You may be locked in a facility for hours during or after the event before the area is sufficiently cleared by law enforcement. Police will sometimes need to go room by room to search for the suspect or to clear the facility for safe passage. Remember, suspects in the past have used improvised explosive devices (IEDs) along their path to death and destruction. This is a matter of safety for law enforcement as well as for the public. Police will need to ensure that when they rescue others, they are not leading them into an area where pre-positioned explosive devices could detonate. If you or others have been injured and require medical attention, keep in mind that before medical first responders can enter to render aid, police need to ensure their safety as well. Therefore, all threats need to be neutralized.

If you have sheltered to hide and are in a group, quickly evaluate who may be able to help should you be required to fight. Quickly decide who will do what and in what order. For example, you will disarm the shooter and then someone else will incapacitate the shooter.

Physically engaging with an active shooter is a last resort. You should only do so when you have no other option and your life is in danger because the shooter is about to enter your concealed area or hiding place. In this circumstance, failing to physically engage the shooter will place your life squarely in the hands of the shooter, and you can only hope that they decide to spare your life.

If you have hidden inside a room, you (and potentially your team) should line up against the side of the wall nearest to the door where you expect the shooter to enter. Stay low, in a position similar to a sprinter's ready position. You should be ready to take action as soon as the shooter enters the room. Take great care to avoid being shot through the wall. Remember, there is no such thing as a fair fight with an active shooter.

The shooter/assailant will have to enter the room either head-first or weapon-first. As soon as the shooter's head or the muzzle of the firearm enters the room, suddenly and with great surprise, launch a violent counterattack. Use the appropriate physical technique to disarm and disable the shooter with a relentless counterattack. This requires total commitment on your part.

Be aware that the shooter may be armed with more than one weapon or may have an accomplice. It is imperative that the shooter be quickly incapacitated to prevent further harm to innocent lives. Keep in mind that active shooters have evolved in their tactics, and there is no neat profile of what an active shooter will or won't do.

If you are successful in disarming an active shooter or use a weapon in your attempt, it will not be clear to responding law enforcement that you are not the actual shooter. Your safety will be at risk if you are in possession of any weapon when they arrive, as it represents an immediate threat to those around you. Be aware of this, and make sure that you have no weapons in your immediate possession when law enforcement arrives.

In some cases, the shooting event occurs when immediate escape is not a viable option. This is referred to as being caught out in the open. Consider taking the following steps in such a situation:

1. Take immediate cover behind something that could stop bullets.
2. Determine the location of the shooter.

3. Locate and utilize an immediate escape route from the entire area.

4. If an escape route is not immediately available, determine a location where you can shelter. The shelter location might be inside a room of some type that should offer you the ability to adequately defend yourself should the shooter breach that location.

5. Stay behind cover and, if the opportunity presents itself, move to a better shelter location. The movement of the shooter through your location may offer an opportunity to move undetected.

6. If the shooter should close the distance between you, or you use cover and surprise to close the distance between you and the shooter, you should be able to disarm and disable the shooter once they move into maximum critical distance (three feet).

Escape

In any shooting, the first thing to do is to utilize the things that are within your immediate control, which hopefully will be to escape the entire area. An active shooter can only kill those who are within the kill zone. When you escape the entire area, you are no longer present in the kill zone and the chance of being injured or killed decreases exponentially. Train your brain to react so that, once danger is confirmed or shots have been fired, you will also immediately transition into action.

In escaping, you should always know several ways to escape your immediate area. There are two different types of exits from any building: conventional and unconventional.

Conventional exits are normal means of exiting and entering a building, such as doors. You should always know at least two different doors to exit any facility. Public places will usually mark doors and emergency doors with signs. Whenever you enter into any type of building (restaurant, movie theater, shopping mall, etc.), ensure that you make note of where the exits are.

Unconventional exits are exits from a place that require breaking out, such as windows and drywall. Take note of heavy items that may be used to break through the glass to make your escape. During a 1991 shooting at Luby's Cafeteria, a patron of the restaurant threw himself through a plate-glass window. Although he sustained injuries by doing so, he also created an escape route for himself and other customers.

Take the time to examine areas you typically frequent, such as your workplace and places of recreation, to provide you with advanced information for escaping and sheltering, should you someday need it. Advance scouting of those areas will help you determine which hallways lead to exterior doors and what places you could use as temporary cover until you can safely evacuate.

During your escape, the primary purpose is to get out fast and alive. This is not the time to multitask by attempting to contact friends or family, to call authorities, or to return to an area to retrieve personal belongings. Take care not to injure yourself by performing exceptional physical feats that will prevent you from continuing your escape. Leaping down a flight of stairs or from a second story may immediately get you out of an area, but will it allow you to continue your escape? Do not jeopardize your escape efforts by sustaining a debilitating injury that will affect your ability to completely escape the kill zone.

If possible, having the exact or approximate location of the shooter is vitally important.

As an example, if you know the shooter is on the north end of your building, you know that you can safely exit from the other side of the building. However, if you don't know the approximate location of the shooter and you are attempting to evacuate, don't blindly run through areas where the shooter could be hiding and waiting to shoot additional victims. With the plethora of police shows on TV, you too can mimic how to tactically evacuate an area when you don't know exactly where the danger is lurking. Although some police shows are better than others, ask your friendly neighborhood cops which show they believe represents the most accurate police tactics. Then you can watch the show to see how the officers "sneak and peak" through an office area or down a hallway.

If you end up evacuating a building and going out into a parking lot, quickly make a left or right turn away from the building door and run toward parked vehicles. The longer you are out in the open, the more you are a target to anyone who may wish to shoot at you as you are escaping. Quickly maneuver between the vehicles in the parking lot and stay as low as possible, putting as much distance as possible between you and the last known location of the shooter. Those vehicles will act as solid cover for you while you escape. Remember, once you escape the kill zone, don't stop until you have put at least one additional building between you and the last known location of the shooter.

Once that is accomplished, it is safe for you to stop, catch your breath, and notify the proper authorities. You may use this time to notify your loved ones and let them know of the danger you experienced and that you are okay.

Always consider that all the information and the true motives of the active shooter may not be readily apparent and may not be known for some time. It should never be assumed that a shooter is just a lone assailant with a specific target in mind.

In fact, with events unfolding around the world that involve the activity of terrorists, it would always be a better assumption that the event could last for several days and include a massive loss of life. Therefore, if you can escape from the entire area, do so. Taking the time out to hide should only be a viable option if your total escape is not possible. As soon as it is safe to escape the danger area, seek avenues to escape and take the necessary actions to maximize your safety.

Sheltering to Hide Indoors

This has proven to be another method of reducing the casualty rate of an active shooter. I advocate the use of this tactic for people who are unable to immediately escape, people who are unwilling or unable to use other options for their survival, or when the other options for survival are not readily available. For the very young, the very old, and those who know that they could never fight should the shooter breach their hiding places, sheltering to hide is an alternative to confronting the armed assailant.

In rare cases, potential victims have had to hide among casualties and "play dead" in order to escape further harm. This tactic is not a preferred method of mitigating an active shooter, but has been used in the past. However, if this choice is the only option available to prevent being immediately shot, it is a choice. I am not in favor of this tactic, as it places the victim's life in the hands of the shooter. However, if that is what is necessary to survive, do it.

One shooting event that illustrates mixing among the casualties occurred on October 15, 1991, in Killeen, Texas, at a Luby's Cafeteria. The shooter was described by others as angry and withdrawn, with a dislike of women. He intentionally crashed his vehicle into the restaurant's front window and exited his vehicle yelling that this was what Bell County had done to him.

He then began shooting at the approximately 140 restaurant patrons and staff. The shooter stalked, shot, and killed twenty-three people, ten of them with a single shot to the head, driven by an intense hostility toward women. People who survived the massacre said the shooter passed over men to shoot women. The shooter said that all women of Killeen and Belton (cities in that area of Texas) were vipers. Media reports given by some of the survivors of the massacre state that some of them hid from the shooter amongst the other victims who had already been shot.

When electing to shelter and hide, be prepared to remain in the hiding place until rescued by responding law enforcement officers or to move to another hiding place if it no longer appears safe. You should also take the opportunity to escape from the entire area if that option becomes possible. If you have a choice, select a hiding place that offers more than one way out. The least desirable choice would be a room (such as a broom closet or restroom) that only has one door and no exterior windows to provide an escape to the outside should the shooter attempt to breach the hiding place.

Once a hiding place is chosen, take whatever steps you can to lock and barricade all doors to keep the shooter from entering that location. Moving objects in front of the door to prevent the door from opening may also provide some shelter if the shooter decides to shoot into that room. Objects like tables, chairs, filing cabinets, and desks can be used to accomplish this task. Stay quiet, silence your cell phone, stay low to the floor, and move far away from the door.

You can proactively "target harden" a room by reinforcing the walls along- side and closest to the door with steel and concealing that reinforcement with drywall. The reinforcement should be sufficiently thick to stop incoming bullets and should extend from the floor to a height of at least four feet. These reinforced areas would be the optimum location for people sheltering inside the room.

Those who choose to "shelter to hide" should spread out and be as quiet as possible to avoid detection.

Most shooters seek a specific target(s) and/or a high body count in a short period of time. Therefore, a shooter who encounters a room where the access has been denied will probably move on to another area in an attempt to obtain easier targets. The shooter may decide to shoot into the room in an attempt to kill those who may be hiding inside. By staying as low as possible, you reduce your chances of being shot.

Students of elementary, middle, and high schools conduct "code yellow" drills where they lock the school classroom doors and shelter in place until given the "all clear." These students have practiced to the point where they are perfectly capable of sheltering and hiding within a classroom.

Once you have sequestered yourself inside a room to shelter and hide, take the time to silently evaluate others. You are looking to see if anyone has any apparent injuries that require immediate, lifesaving first aid. You are also evaluating others in the room to see if they may pose a potential threat. In one case, a high school had reason to lock down due to a report of a potentially armed student on their campus. When teachers receive word of a lockdown, they will look into the hallway and have any students in the hallway come into their classroom, whether or not the student is assigned to that class during that time period. As the school police continued their search for the potentially armed student, they eventually performed a room-to-room search, only to discover that the potentially armed student they were looking for had already and inadvertently (as per school policy) been sequestered inside a classroom, sheltering along with the other people inside.

None of the people inside that room were aware of the threat that student posed to their safety. The room occupants were quite flabbergasted when they learned that the person they were sheltering from had been present with them the entire time.

Once you have evaluated others who have sheltered there with you, take the time to give yourself a brief once-over. You are checking to ensure that you have not been seriously injured during the initial escape. Shock may elevate your adrenalin level to the point where you may be unaware that you have sustained an injury until your body has had the chance to relax.

In the near future, most emergency communication centers should be able to receive text messages from people involved in an active shooting. Unfortunately, as of writing, not all agencies have this capability. You should contact your local emergency communications center and inquire whether or not they can receive emergency text messages. If the agency is not yet set up for text messages, notification to law enforcement about an active shooter may be relegated to a vocal conversation with an emergency communications dispatcher.

Designate only one person (typically one of the calmest people in the room) to quietly call 911 to report the shooting. With one person calling the authorities, you will avoid duplication of effort, reduce the amount of noise in the room, and reduce the risk of overwhelming the 911 operator. Provide a physical description of the shooter(s), including ethnicity, gender, height, weight, clothing description, the person's identity (if known), and last known location. If possible, advise the operator as to the type of weapon(s) the shooter(s) may have and the condition of any known victims. This information will assist responding officers in taking the appropriate steps to engage the shooter. If you are unable to describe the shooter, never put yourself or others at risk in order to obtain such information.

The mere fact that a shooter is at a particular location will be sufficient to send multiple police resources to address the threat.

Take this time to text your loved ones and notify them of your status and location. It is vitally important that you tell your loved ones to stay clear of the area and resist the urge to rush to the scene to reunite with you once you have been rescued. The rescue effort could take a matter of minutes, hours, or even days. Also, if your loved ones arrive in the area, they may be placed in danger as well as forcing law enforcement to ensure their safety as they establish crowd control for the area. This gives police one more thing to deal with instead of using their resources to provide your rescue.

During a January 25, 2014, mall shooting in Columbia, Maryland, I listened to a radio station that provided its listeners with the most current information about the shooting. More than one person was still on scene and locked down inside one of the businesses. One person had called a radio station and was giving her interview about what she had experienced during the shooting and her current status at her location. I would never recommend doing any media interview while still waiting to be rescued by police.

Sheltering to Hide Outdoors

If the shooting occurs while you are outdoors, the first initial reaction should be the same as when a shooting occurs inside a building: take evasive action and get down behind something that can stop bullets. The idea is to make yourself a smaller target by getting as low as possible and using a large object to temporarily shield yourself. You are also attempting to conceal yourself from the view of the shooter. Concrete walls are excellent in providing cover from bullets.

You then want to determine the direction the shots are being fired from and the location of the shooter. Until you can determine if the shots are coming toward you, stay where you are until you can move to a safer location. You may need to move while staying as low as possible, perhaps even crouched down or on your hands and feet.

If you are among vehicles, move between them, as they will both shield you from bullets and conceal you from the view of the shooter. If you are using a car, truck, or other large vehicle as solid cover, stay behind the wheels of the vehicle to offer the best protection. The steel components of the wheel assembly will provide the best protection. You also want to avoid crouching in the open space between the wheels. Crouching in those open areas allows the possibility of the shooter bouncing or skipping bullets off the pavement (intentionally or inadvertently) and hitting you. Avoid sticking your head up over the top of the vehicle, through the glass, or around the vehicle to look around.

Using a vehicle for cover—side to side

Using a vehicle for cover—front to back

As long as you are safe, stay behind solid cover. Be prepared to move to a different location, either to escape from the area or to find new cover should the shooter change locations. Stay as low as possible, move further away from the shooter, and remember to move between vehicles using them as cover until you can safely escape the area.

Sheltering to Hide Inside a Vehicle

There have been occasions when a motorist unwittingly drives into a kill zone. On December 9, 2011, a gunman walked down the middle of a street in Hollywood, California, shooting at passing cars. The shooter fired at least nine shots into the air and at passing cars. The gunman shouted, "Kill me" and "I'm gonna die." A witness captured video of the gunman from a window several stories above the street. He shouted down at the shooter, attempting to distract him and draw his attention away from the people on the street. The gunman ran out of ammunition for his handgun and pulled a knife. Police officers responded and shot and killed the gunman (CBS Los Angeles, December 9, 2011).

If you are driving toward the shooter, you have several options:

- Stop, turn around, and quickly drive in the opposite direction.
- Stop, place your car in reverse, and drive in the opposite direction.
- Duck down as low as possible toward the center of the vehicle, speed up, and drive past the shooter, exiting the kill zone.
- Duck down as low as possible toward the center of the vehicle, speed up, and using your vehicle as a weapon, strike the shooter with your vehicle.

If your vehicle is not in motion and you are a significant distance from where the shooting is taking place, you should do the following:

- Duck down as low as possible toward the center of the vehicle and drive out of the kill zone.

If your vehicle is unable to move or is blocked by other traffic at the location where the shooting is occurring, you can do this:

- Duck down as low as possible toward the center of the vehicle, open up a door farthest from the shooter, move to the exterior of the vehicle, and use the applicable portions of the vehicle as cover.
- Duck down as low as possible toward the center of the vehicle, open up a door farthest from the shooter, move to the exterior of the vehicle, and staying as low as possible, escape from the area on foot.

If you are riding a motorcycle, your options for survival are more limited. You should either escape the kill zone or use nearby cars as cover to hide behind.

Staying inside your vehicle and hoping the shooter does not move in your direction places you in the same physical and mental condition as hiding in a closet. If the shooter elects to move toward your vehicle and open fire on you, you will be in a confined space, and your ability to survive the shooting will now be dependent solely on the shooter. Therefore, the longer you stay at the location, the more your life is at risk.

Attacks using a motor vehicle throughout Europe and the United States are occurring with greater frequency. In these cases, the driver uses a vehicle to strike, run over or run down innocent unsuspecting pedestrians with the intent to kill them. Some of the most recent cases include:

History:

- On the Ohio State Campus on November 28, 2016, a car struck several people and when the driver exited he used a knife to continue his attack. A total of 13 people were hospitalized for their injuries.

- In Berlin Germany on December 19, 2016, twelve people were killed when a person intentionally drove a tractor-trailer into a crowd of people at a Christmas event.
- At the Westminster Bridge near Parliament on March 22, 2017 a driver used a sport utility vehicle to drive into pedestrians, killing two people and injuring many others. The driver fled on foot and approached Parliament. The lone assailant stabbed an unarmed police officer to death.
- And on April 7, 2017, four people were killed and 15 injured when a stolen truck was intentionally driven into a crowd of shoppers in Stockholm, Sweden. The driver fled the scene only to be captured by police days later.

These types of attacks have one single purpose. In some cases (not all of which are listed in this work) after the vehicular attack, the assailant has exited their vehicle and continued to kill by means of a firearm, an edged weapon or Improvised Explosive Devices.

Some experts attempt to determine if the attack was committed by a Terrorist or a mentally ill person. The motivation of the attacker is not as important as ensuring the potential victims have the best available information, tactics and techniques available to save their lives during such an attack.

Response strategies for Business/Government:

One proactive deterrent that can be used is to deploy steel stanchions in places where large numbers of pedestrians have the most probability of gathering and traversing. In such areas, the local jurisdiction may have already dedicated that area for pedestrian foot traffic only. Each stanchion would be encased in concrete and spaced to facilitate the flow of pedestrian foot traffic, but prevent the entry of motor vehicles (cars, trucks and busses). Another measure is to increase the visible presence of uniformed police officers within those heavily populated pedestrian areas. The uniformed officers would be armed with long guns (semi-automatic rifles, shotguns using slugs or a combination of both) that would sufficiently penetrate the driver's compartment of any vehicle attempting to be used in killing innocent pedestrians. Law enforcement can also employ spike strips to flatten tires once a suspected vehicle is in motion. There should also be a public safety campaign to educate all citizens on how to best assist law enforcement and avoid friendly fire by officers should the need arise to respond and use deadly force to stop such an event.

Citizen response strategies:

One of the first things people can do to reduce the potential of becoming a victim to this type of murderous activity rest in their ability to be <u>totally aware of the entire surroundings</u> anytime they are in public areas. Staying alert to the sounds of people screaming (in panic, while they are escaping or because they have already been victimized by this madness). Notice the sounds of any vehicle's engine accelerating or traveling at a high rate of speed, the sounds of a vehicle colliding with other objects (such as another vehicle or other heavy objects) or driving within areas where vehicles are not intended to be traversed by anything other than pedestrians.

Anytime you feels you need to escape such a environment, remember you are on foot and the possibility of outrunning a fast moving motor vehicle are limited. Use angles to assist in your escape. As an example, if the vehicle is driving north towards you, do not continue to move in a northerly direction in an attempt to outrun the vehicle. Instead, a better option may be to move 90 degrees (east or west) from the vehicle's oncoming path of destruction. Moving to the inside of a building by using a door (or entering via a broken window) may offer a quick escape location. Use objects that won't easily be run over for temporary cover while continuing to escape. Some cities use large 50 gallon size flower pots for their area beautification. Those large flower pots may not totally stop a speeding vehicle, but may provide just the opportunity to slow the vehicle down while engaged in escaping from the path of the vehicle.

Ascending upwards out of the path of a vehicle can also be considered. When no other options for escape appear available, quickly climbing high enough up a large tree, a light pole, a traffic standard/ signal or telephone pole might be another avenue for escape if that is the only option available if you are caught totally out in the open. Always have a plan no matter where you are! Take a couple of seconds to consider (prior to such an attack ever occurring) that if you had to escape what and where would your best options be. Play the game of "what if." The next time you are out and about on foot, stop in a safe place and take a few moments to ask yourself, "if" you had to move out of the path of an oncoming vehicle, which routes would conceivably work best for your survival.

For the legally armed defender/citizen, using a firearm to shoot at a driver or a vehicle with the intent of disabling the driver or the vehicle who is attempting to run you over is not the best strategy and there are more disadvantages than advantages. For an armed citizen to take their best shot at the driver who is determined to run them over, the armed citizen would need to be in a stationary position. Being in that stationary position will more than likely place the armed citizen in the path of that on- coming vehicle for a longer period of time and increases the possibility of being struck by that vehicle. If the armed citizen is attempting to shoot while on the move (running away from the vehicle) the chances of hitting the driver or the potential vulnerable areas of the vehicle decreases and the chances of the rounds fired by the legally armed defender striking unintended targets (other innocent people) increases. Shooting at a moving vehicle may not have the same effects it has in a Hollywood movie. The bottom line is for people caught in the melee of such a vehicle attack, using a firearm to shoot and successfully hit the assailant driver or any portion of the assailant's vehicle in an attempt to disable the vehicle is extremely difficult at best. The time may be better served by escaping from the carnage.

Sheltering to Fight

This is an option when escape is not possible, or when you have sheltered to hide and the shooter is about to breach your location. This is a last-resort effort when your life is in immediate danger.

Any face-to-face encounter with an armed assailant is extremely dangerous, especially if the defender is not armed and must depend on physical techniques to overcome the shooter. The best option mandates that if you are alone and you have decided to take action, you will already know what to do, how to do it, and when to execute your practiced techniques. You must have the physical ability to disarm the shooter, the mental preparedness to fight for your life, and the mental toughness to know that you may need to take a human life to save your own life.

When you are using a technique to disarm an armed assailant, the movements need to be economical and efficient. The technique should not require more than two moves to remove the firearm from the hands of the armed assailant and place it into the full control of the defender. With diligent practice and significant repetition, these two moves can be easily done and will prove invaluable should you find yourself in this situation. The principle is an easy one: if the shooter's weapon is taken away, they cannot shoot you with that weapon.

With any firearms disarming techniques, the defender must be within the critical distance (one to three feet) to utilize these lifesaving moves.

For the purposes of "sheltering to fight," the best area to stage is against the wall next to the door knob. Regardless of whether it is one or more defenders who will take on the shooter/assailant, all defenders should be in a line against the wall crouched low in a three point stance similar to a football player on the line waiting for the ball to snap.

All defenders should be looking at the door so that once the door opens, and the shooter/assailant begins to cross the threshold into the room, each defender can immediately launch a counterattack against the shooter/assailant. The first defender should be designated to disarm the shooter/assailant of their weapon. Other defenders can then disable the shooter/assailant by applying a carotid hold or other methods using improvised weapons. If there is only one defender, the priority will be to disarm the shooter/assailant of their weapon and incapacitate them. Disarming the shooter/assailant can be accomplished by using a weapon disarming technique. If the lone defender is either not capable or confident of physically disarming the shooter/assailant, the defender may use any number of methods to disable the shooter/assailant.

One method is to use an improvised weapon such as a medium size rock, brick, or other blunt object to strike the assailant in the head with sufficient force that will cause the offender to lose consciousness. Another method is to use a sharp object (paper cutter blade, scissors, etc.) to stab the assailant in the throat.

Consider that after the defender launches a counter attack, the offender may not immediately be neutralized and continued effort may be required. In all instances, ensure that the weapon of the offender is accounted for and does not place yourself or others inside the room in unnecessary peril.

The two most important aspects of a successful firearm disarming technique are to immediately deflect the weapon (by moving the barrel of the firearm away from the defender with one hand) and, once that is accomplished, to disarm the shooter and place the weapon in the hands of the defender (by using both hands to remove the weapon).The defender should then be capable of using that firearm to return fire if required. The process should not take longer than one to two seconds before the shooter is fully disarmed and the firearm is in the hands of the defender.

The weapons disarm should be executed as soon as the muzzle of the firearm enters the room. If you are with others who can assist you, quickly and quietly designate which person will take specific actions in your defensive group. This will make your fight for survival much more efficient, without duplication of effort and loss of valuable time. Align your defensive group in a single file line along the wall immediately adjacent to the entrance you expect the shooter to enter.

The person who will perform the weapons disarm should be at the head of the line. If you are alone, you should occupy the same position to disarm the shooter. The next person in the line is the person who will quickly move to the rear of the shooter and incapacitate them with a carotid hold. The entire counterattack should last no more than fifteen seconds from the disarming (one to two seconds) through to the incapacitation of the shooter (five to ten seconds).

Prepare months or years in advance by learning proper firearms and weapons disarming techniques. Make sure that when learning or practicing with any firearm disarming technique, you never use a loaded firearm. In addition, all edged weapons should be appropriately altered to prevent injury during practice sessions. There is no substitute for being prepared should these techniques be necessary. If you have decided to practice these techniques with friends, family members, or coworkers, each person should be fully capable of performing any one of these actions.

Critical Distances

Usually, shooters choose to engage targets that are relatively close to them. For a suspect armed with an edged weapon, the critical distance will be one to two feet between the suspect and victim. For a suspect who is armed with a handgun, the distance moves outward from point-blank range (within one to two feet). The distance at which a person can be accurate with a handgun is contingent upon the shooter's ability. A person who applies diligent practice with a handgun can increase proficiency and thus successfully engage targets farther away. For shooters who use long guns, the range can be over a thousand feet. The following chart will describe the minimum and maximum effective ranges of edged weapons and various firearms:

Knife/sword/axe/hatchet	0 to 4 feet
Handgun	0 to 150 feet
Shotgun (pellets)	0 to 120 feet
Shotgun (slugs)	0 to 150 feet
Assault rifle	0 to 1140 feet

In order for a defender to effectively utilize a lifesaving movement using physical techniques, the defender must be within three feet of the shooter. Being aware of the critical distances of the various weapons allows the defender to decide whether to stay within that potential kill zone and execute a defensive technique. If the defender is outside of the three-foot critical distance required to execute a physical disarming technique, the defender has two options: either find a way to quickly close the distance and physically engage the shooter, or flee the area and exit the kill zone. Once outside of the kill zone, the defender may either shelter to hide or shelter to fight.

Handgun Disarms

The best position to approach and disarm an armed assailant is at an angle, ideally 45 to 90 degrees. It would be preferable if the shooter is not yet pointing the weapon directly at the defender, although this is not always the case. Although the following instructions and illustrations show the defender standing directly in front of the assailant, this is actually the most dangerous and least desirable position.

In the case of a handgun disarm of a right-handed shooter, the defender should use their left hand to grab the back of the shooter's gun hand. The defender should move the weapon approximately ten inches to their right. In all cases, the gun barrel must clear the right side of the defender's body (but go no further).

The defender then places their right hand underneath and around the middle portion of the handgun and rotates the handgun's barrel toward the shooter's head in a small counterclockwise circular motion.

This places the shooter's right gun hand in a reverse wristlock position and weakens the shooter's ability to hold onto the weapon with any strength.

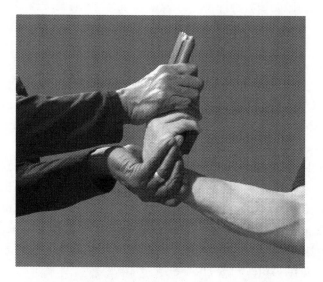

Once the barrel of the handgun has been pointed toward the shooter's face using a small circular motion, the handgun is primed to be **pushed, never pulled** from the shooter's hand. Pulling the handgun out of the shooter's hand could cause a round to be discharged.

Once the shooter has been successfully disarmed, the defender must step away and physically disengage in order to be prepared to use that weapon against the shooter if further force is attempted by the shooter. A firearm disarming technique should never take more than two movements before the weapon is out of the hands of the assailant.

Long Gun Disarms

In the case of a long gun (like a shotgun or rifle) disarm of a right-handed shooter, in which their right hand is on the trigger and their left hand is near the barrel, the defender will use their right hand to push the barrel to the defender's right, so that it does not point at them. The defender should then grip the barrel of the long gun with their right hand, with the palm facing toward them. The defender will then reach over the top of the long gun with their left hand and grab the weapon roughly between the stock and the trigger, while taking a small step toward the left side of the shooter.

Move the barrel in a small circular motion to the right and then upward, violently striking the shooter in the face with the barrel of the long gun. Continue moving the barrel of the weapon downward in a diagonal line (from upper right to lower left) to completely disarm the shooter.

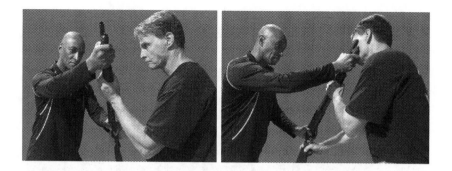

Once the long gun has been dislodged from the shooter's hands, disengage from the shooter by taking a slight step backward. You may use the shooter's own weapon against the shooter if they attempt a further assault.

Secured Long Gun Disarm

In the event that the shooter has the weapon secured to their body using a sling or other device, total separation between the suspect and the primary weapon may be very difficult without the help of another person.

If you do have another person to assist you, one person handles the weapon while the second person is designated to physically incapacitate the shooter.

The initial contact should always be the person who will handle the weapon. Using their right hand, the defender will sweep the barrel toward the defender's right. They should then grip the barrel of the long gun with their right hand, with the palm facing toward them. The defender will place the barrel deep into the inside crook of their right elbow in a cradle fashion. The defender will use their left hand to reach under the long gun and grab the weapon roughly between the stock and the trigger. The defender will then move the stock into the inside crook of their left elbow in a cradle fashion. The defender will then bring both arms close to their body and cradle the weapon flat against their chest.

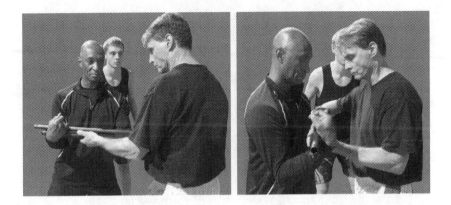

Once the weapon is secured in that fashion, the second person will incapacitate the shooter with a carotid hold. Once the shooter is neutralized, the weapon needs to be removed (if possible) from the shooter.

These techniques, when described in great detail, appear to be a number of movements. But in actuality, there are only two movements: move the gun barrel away so that it does not point at the defender and take the weapon away from the shooter. It is imperative that the disarming technique not just deflect, but totally dislodge and disarm the shooter from the firearm and expeditiously place the firearm in the hands of the defender, who can be immediately capable of shooting the assailant if need be. Anyone who feels that they may need to someday use a firearms disarming technique to save their life needs to devote adequate time to ensuring that the technique is easy to perform. You may only get one chance to utilize this movement. You want it done right the first time.

Weapons Disarming Priorities

In the event that an assailant is armed with a weapon in each hand, the below list provides instructions on which weapon should be addressed first in order to minimize the potential for harm:

- Two handguns: The defender should choose the handgun closest to them. Once the first handgun is disarmed, the defender must use it against the shooter to stop all further aggression.
- One handgun and one long gun: The defender should stay well inside the range where the shooter would find it most difficult to aim a long gun at the defender. The defender should disarm the shooter of the handgun and then use it to stop all further aggression.
- Two long guns: The defender should choose the long gun closest to them. Once the long gun is disarmed, the defender must use it to stop all further aggression.
- One handgun and one knife: The defender should choose the handgun. Once the handgun is disarmed, the defender must use it to stop all further aggression.
- One long gun and one knife: The defender should choose the long gun. Once the long gun is disarmed, the defender must use it to stop all further aggression.

- Two knives: The defender should choose the knife closest to them. Once the knife is disarmed, the defender must use force to stop all further aggression.

Carotid Control

If there is another person to assist in the shelter and fight option, that person may place the assailant in a carotid hold. Begin by standing completely to the rear of the assailant. Place your right arm around the neck and underneath the jaw line. Place your right palm on your left bicep. Place your left palm on the back of the assailant's head. Conceal your face in the inner crook of your left arm (bracing arm) where your hand and bicep meet. Continuously push the assailant's head and neck forward with the left hand while simultaneously squeezing the front of the assailant's neck with your right arm. Finish the hold by moving your feet apart and pulling your assailant backward to force them into a seated position. Taking your assailant to the ground prevents you from being flipped over the top of the assailant's head and ending up on your back.

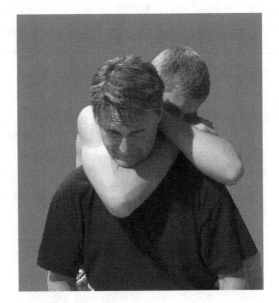

With this hold, you will have temporary and total control over your assailant. Do not remove your hold on the subject until he/she is unconscious. Releasing the pressure from the hold will weaken its integrity and possibly allow the assailant to escape. The assailant should lose consciousness after five to fifteen seconds. Do not be concerned if the assailant begins tugging, pulling down, or attempting to move the front (choking) arm. Attempting to remove the choking arm indicates that the assailant does not know how to escape this hold (which is actually done by first removing the bracing hand/arm). Ensure that you render the assailant unconscious and do not release the hold until that person is incapacitated.

If you elect to use improvised weapons that are easily found within your location, chose something heavy to strike the shooter. It is important that you do have control over your improvised weapon and do not strike any unintended target, such as your fellow defenders.

Use an instrument like the bottom of a fire extinguisher to strike the shooter in the face or head with sufficient force to render them unconscious. Use other items such as chairs, rocks, or heavy pipes that may also be found within your sheltering area.

Edged Weapons Disarms

In several cases, assailants have been armed with edged weapons. On April 9, 2014, a student at a high school in Murrysville, Pennsylvania, used two knives to stab and slash over twenty fellow students before he was subdued by others. Another event occurred on an Amtrak train on December 5, 2014, where a man who had been acting strangely suddenly stabbed four people with a knife.

Police were previously summoned because the man was acting suspiciously. Police located the stabbing suspect and used a Taser to take him into custody. Fortunately, no deaths resulted from either event. In another situation, on October 23, 2014 a man attacked four New York City Police Officers with a hatchet as the officers posed for a photograph in Queens, New York. And yet, on September 17, 2016 a man dressed in a private security officer's uniform attacked and at least 9 people in a knife rampage at the Crossroads Mall in St. Cloud, Minnesota. An off-duty police officer shot and killed the attacker.

The majority of face to face edged weapons attacks occur in a stabbing, slicing/swinging or chopping motion. Although there may be slight variations, an assailant will usually hold a knife with the blade protruding between the thumb and index finger (illustrated as position 1), or with the knife blade protruding from the bottom of the hand (illustrated as position 2).

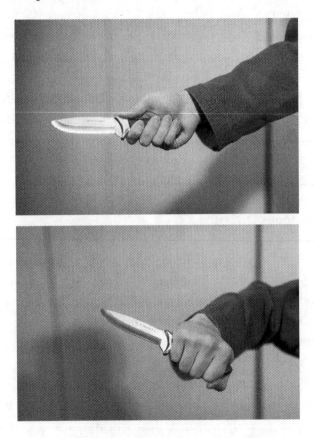

In the case of a hatchet, meat cleaver or other similar weapon, the assailant will typically hold the weapon by the handle, with the handle extending outward protruding from the index finger and thumb where they attack in a chopping/swinging motion.

For the safety of both individuals when practicing these edged weapons defensive techniques, **never** practice with a knife that is sharp along the blade or at the point. This allows both participants to practice these techniques without fear of significant injury. Speed and proficiency only develop after multiple practice session.

There are a number of strategies to defend against an edged weapons attack, but only two strategies will be illustrated for the edged weapons defense techniques in this book. The **first strategy** is to re-direct the edged weapon attack to allow the momentum of the assailant's strike to carry them in a continuous motion along a new path; step into the assailant capturing both of their legs, throw them to the ground and to disable/disarm the assailant.

Once the assailant has been forcefully thrown to the ground, disable the assailant by delivering a foot stomp (using the heel of the foot) to the head of the assailant to render him/her unconscious and then complete the weapons disarm.

When executing a knife disarm while the weapon held in position 1 (with the cutting edges protruding from the area nearest the thumb and index finger), the weapon is forced from the hand between the thumb and index finger. The defender will apply pressure at the hilt of the knife (or handle of the axe/hatchet) and prying the weapon starting at the assailant's thumb and index finger and move towards the pinky finger. When the assailant is holding the knife/weapon in position 2, the weapon is forced from the base of the assailant's hand starting near their pinky finger and moving towards the thumb.

The **second strategy** is _utilized only for a reverse knife stab aimed at the right side of the defender's head, neck, upper or lower torso_. The assailant is holding the knife in their right hand with the blade protruding from the bottom of their hand, (position 2). This strategy calls for the defender to actually stop the incoming knife momentum and then utilize the other hand to place the assailant's attacking hand into a reverse wrist lock. Only while applying sufficient torque to the reverse wrist lock can the assailant's knife be disarmed.

As with any knife defense and disarming strategy, the movements must be precise as there is a very small margin of error. It is possible that the defender could be injured, cut, or stabbed during the defense sequence. Anytime the defender is engaged in a life and death encounter and sustains a serious injury during the altercation, the defender is even more compelled to expeditiously complete the defensive technique and incapacitate the assailant to prevent a further attack.

After any deadly encounter, the defender should always get away to a place of safety and ascertain/seek treatment for any injury they sustained during the physical altercation.

For ease of explanation, all techniques will be illustrated with the assailant wielding the edged weapon in their right hand. Any defender wishing to gain complete competence against an assailant should practice these defensive techniques using either hand

The re-direction of the attack is performed by <u>guiding and consistently maintaining contact with the hand wielding the weapon</u> in a smooth and continuous motion to either the left or right side of the defender. As the assailant and defender stand face to face, any attack aimed at the left side of the defender will be redirected using the defender's left hand.

When the attack is aimed at the right side of the defender (<u>except for when the defender is holding the knife in position two preparing to attack in a reverse stabbing motion</u>), the defender will use the right hand as the primary re-direction tool. When the attack is aimed towards the center of the defender, the defender may use either hand to as their primary re-direction tool.

Although the description of the technique is explained in several steps, once the defender becomes competent, these steps can be combined with other movements and performed simultaneously. When executing all redirection and throwing techniques, the assailant's arm should move in a smooth and continuous arch from the inception of the strike, through the redirection of the edged weapon to one side of the defender, only ending when the assailant has been thrown to the ground. The time elapsed in this re-direction technique should be no greater than 2 seconds.

This technique is designed to defend against an assailant attacking with the following types of attacks:

- Knife held in position 1 in a "slicing" action aimed at the left side of the head, neck, or upper torso;
- Hatchet held in position 1 in a "chopping" motion aimed at the left side of the head, neck, or upper torso;
- Knife held in position 1 with a stab to the lower torso;
- Knife held in position 2 in a slicing motion, aimed at the left side of the head, neck, or upper torso.

The defender will stand with feet shoulder width apart and both hands held in close to the center of the chest. As the assailant's strike comes near, the defender will move their left hand outward to meet the incoming attack between twelve and sixteen inches away from the defender's head or body.

The defender will use the left hand at the knife edge and outer forearm portion of their forearm to make light contact with the assailant's right wrist area. After the light contact is made, the defender will use their left hand to grab the right wrist area of the assailant to control the wrist and weapon.

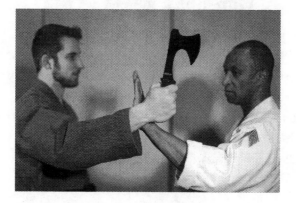

This is the beginning stage of the re-direction and will <u>not stop</u>

<u>the incoming momentum of the assailant's attack</u>, but merely guide and re-direct the attack. The re-direction is intended to keep the assailant's attacking hand and weapon along the left side of the defender throughout the entire technique.

Next, the defender will step into the assailant's body, turning so that their back is against the assailant's torso.

Using the right hand, the defender will reach underneath the assailant's right arm at the shoulder and lock onto the back side of the assailant's right shoulder.

The defender will bend their left knee while keeping the right leg straight which will allow both the assailant's knees to be centered near the defender's right calf and behind the knee.

In order to complete the throw, the defender must have captured **both legs** of the assailant (reference the illustrated photograph). Then, the defender bends forward in a semi-circular fashion at the waist (first slightly towards their center and then sharply over to the left knee) placing their right elbow on the inner side of their bending left knee. As a result, the assailant will be thrown to the ground <u>onto their back</u>.

The defender will use their right foot to deliver a heel stomp to the assailant's head.

After the heel stomp is completed, the assailant may be disarmed from his/her weapon.

This technique is designed to defend against an assailant attacking with the following attacks:

- Knife held in position 1 in a reverse "slicing" motion aimed at the right side of the head, neck, upper or lower torso;
- Hatchet held in position 1 in a "reverse chopping motion" aimed at the right side of the head, neck, or upper torso.

The defender will stand with feet shoulder width apart and both hands held in close to the center of the chest. As the assailant's strike comes near, the defender will move their right hand outward to meet the incoming attack between twelve and sixteen inches away from the defender.

The defender will use the right hand at the knife edge and outer forearm portion of their arm to make light contact with the assailant's right wrist area.

After the light contact is made, the defender will use their right hand to grab the right wrist area of the assailant to control the right wrist and weapon. This is the beginning stage of the re-direction and will not stop the incoming momentum of the assailant's attack, but merely guide and re-direct the attack.

This redirection is intended to keep the assailant's attacking hand and weapon along the right side of the defender throughout the entire technique. Next, the defender will step into the assailant, turning so that their back is facing the assailant's upper torso.

Using the left hand, the defender will reach underneath the assailant's right arm at the shoulder and lock onto the front side of the assailant's right shoulder.

The defender will bend at the right knee while keeping the left knee/leg straight.

In order to complete the throw, the defender must have captured **both legs** of the assailant (reference the illustrated photograph). As a result, the assailant will be <u>thrown to the ground onto their back</u>.

The defender will use their left foot to deliver a heel stomp to the assailant's head.

After the heel stomp is completed, the assailant may be disarmed from his/her knife.

This technique is designed to defend against an assailant attacking with a reverse stab with the knife held in position 2 (<u>the blade protruding from the bottom of the hand</u>):

- Knife aimed at the right side of the head, neck, or upper torso;
- Knife held aimed downwards at the top of the head, face, neck, and upper torso.

With the knife in the assailant's right hand, the assailant attacks with a reverse stabbing motion. The defender will stand with feet shoulder width apart and both hands held in close to the center of the chest.

As the assailant's knife strike comes near, the defender will use the right hand at the knife edge and outer forearm portion of their arm to "block" the incoming knife attack approximately twelve inches away from the defender.

Unlike the previous knife defenses, _the defender must effectively **stop** the momentum of the incoming knife attack_.

Immediately after the block, the defender will use the left hand to reach out and grab the back of the assailant's right knife wielding hand and apply a reverse wrist lock to control the right wrist and weapon.

Because the knife is dangerously close to the blocking hand, the defender must be precise in their hand placement. The defender will apply sufficient torque on the assailant's right wrist into a reverse wrist lock to enable the blade of the knife to move away from the defender's right wrist/arm to allow a safer application of the disarm. Once the wrist lock is fully engaged, the assailant's grip on the weapon should be diminished facilitating the disarming process.

When executing a disarm when the <u>reverse knife stab is aimed high,</u> the assailant's knife is disarmed by first applying a reverse wrist lock to the assailant's right hand and second, using the edge of the right palm against the hilt of the knife, forcing the knife towards the assailant's right pinky finger and moving towards their right thumb and index finger. Ensure that during the disarming process, the right palm is not on the cutting edge of the blade, but on the hilt of the knife!

When executing a disarm when <u>the reverse knife stab is aimed low,</u> the assailant's knife is disarmed by first applying a reverse wrist lock to the assailant's right hand and second, inverting the right hand (turning the thumb side clockwise).

The defender will then be able to place their thumb and index finger at the hilt of the assailant's knife, forcing it towards the assailant's right pinky finger and moving towards their right thumb and index finger.

In both of the reverse stab disarming techniques, once the reverse wrist lock <u>*and takedown*</u> is applied, the knife can be completely removed from the assailant's hand as he/she is forced to fall backwards. It is during the actual takedown that the assailant's knife can be forced into their throat (for all attacks aimed high) or to lower available targets (for all attacks aimed low).

Defensive Improvised Environmental Weapons

Inside most elementary schools are large paper cutters that usually have a twenty-inch blade held on by a single bolt. The blade of the paper cutter has a handle on one end. Teachers could ascertain the size of the bolt that secures the blade to the paper cutter and have a wrench readily available and conveniently kept inside the teacher's desk. If an emergency occurs, the teacher could obtain the wrench from their desk drawer, remove the blade from the cutting board, and use the blade as a machete against the active shooter should the classroom be breached.

If you always use the same office or room at your place of work, obtain a sizable rock or brick that can be held in one hand and wielded without too much discomfort. Paint a brief quote on the rock and use it as a paperweight or doorstop. In the event that a shooter breaches that room, that object may be used to strike the assailant in the head and disable them.

The shooter will have to enter a room either headfirst (looking before entering the room) or weapon first. The defender could use sufficient force to strike into that vulnerable area (either neck or wrist) to incapacitate the assailant. Understand that it might take multiple strikes to fully incapacitate the assailant. Using either weapon would obviously be deemed as a justifiable use of force to save your life or the lives of others sheltered there with you.

Tactical Errors

Never use an ineffective physical technique to disarm an active shooter. As an experienced martial arts teacher and practitioner, I have seen a variety of handgun disarms that are practical, easy to apply, and effective in disarming the assailant. I have also seen a number of techniques that are highly ineffective and only serve to place the defender at greater risk. In the Panama City, Florida, school board shooting in December 2010, a woman attempted to use her purse to knock the gun from the assailant's hand. When her effort failed, the shooter turned his attention to her. Luckily, the shooter spared her life. This real-life video illustrates how an honorable effort can fail due to a lack of proper training in handgun disarms. The shooter, for whatever reason, chose not to punish the woman for her failed gun disarm and eventually continued with his attack on the school board. The shooter ultimately committed suicide.

Never leave shelter or cover while the shooter may still be a threat. If you cannot see that the shooter has been incapacitated, stay in a safe location. Only leave if you are compelled to escape via a known safe route or are rescued by law enforcement.

Use extreme caution if you open a locked or barricaded door. If you have sheltered inside a room, do not open the door to allow a person in whose identity you cannot verify. It can be difficult to know if the person attempting to get inside is a potential victim seeking shelter, law enforcement attempting to rescue you, or the shooter trying to gain entrance in order to kill more victims. This is a tough decision and one in which you need to consider all the information available to you at the time.

If you are not sure of the person's identity, don't open the door until you can verify whether they are a threat. If police are on the scene, you can always call 911 to verify that the officers are at that particular door. If the door has a master key, the authorities will be able to open the door themselves. If you believe the person attempting entry is a potential victim, listen to the tone of their voice. If the person belongs to the environment, ask a couple of simple questions that will allow you to verify their identity. If you have any doubt, you can choose to open the door and be prepared to unleash a violent counterattack if they are actually the shooter.

Once the shooter has been neutralized, do not pick up the discarded weapon. Regardless of how the shooter was neutralized, do not pick up any dropped or discarded weapons. By picking up that firearm, responding law enforcement will see you as the threat and may begin shooting at you. Additionally, that firearm may provide forensic evidence that law enforcement will need for their investigations. Allow authorities to handle any evidence at the crime scene. You don't want your fingerprints on that weapon.

Legally Armed Defenders

If you have a permit for a concealed firearm, are physically trained and emotionally prepared, and have the appropriate mindset, you can surprise and incapacitate the shooter. You should only do so when the shooter has either presented themselves, is in the act of breaching your hiding place, or is approaching your location.

Necessary Equipment for All Who Carry Concealed Firearms

For all legally armed individuals who carry a firearm within an area where an active shooting could occur, the following equipment should be readily available every time:

- The weapon of choice that you are the most competent with and can safely conceal on your person
- Extra ammunition
- A small, fully charged tactical flashlight
- A fully charged cell phone
- A hands-free Bluetooth device for your phone

Your choice of clothing may also be a factor in carrying and concealing the above items. The cell phone should be somewhere immediately accessible. The Bluetooth device can be worn on the ear but does not have to be turned on unless a phone call is being made or received. This will save the battery life of the device should you need to use it while involved with an armed assailant.

Mindset of the Legally Armed Defender

Remember that your body will respond to a life-death emergency with adrenalin. That adrenalin will have an effect on how your mind and body respond to that emergency. You must factor that into your defensive strategies in order to succeed.

Just because you were successful in engaging the shooter and your shot struck them, this does not mean that the fight is over. Depending on where, and how many times, the shooter was shot, they may still be able to continue the deadly rampage. There is no such thing as a fair fight with an active shooter. Therefore, using verbal warnings will only give the shooter advance warning that you are present and possibly prepared to use deadly force. Also, announcing anything to the shooter takes away any and all tactical elements of surprise and places the shooter at a greater advantage and the defender at a disadvantage.

An example of verbal warning going wrong occurred on November 20, 2005, at a mall in Tacoma, Washington. A twenty-year-old gunman entered the mall with a semi-automatic rifle and a handgun and began shooting people. A legally armed citizen decided to intervene and readied his own semi-automatic firearm, telling the shooter to put down his gun. The shooter responded by shooting the legally armed citizen five times. The shooter stayed inside the mall, entered a store, and took several hostages. The shooter ultimately surrendered to Tacoma police several hours later. According to media reports, there was one other legally armed citizen in the mall at the time of the attack who did not fire at the shooter for fear of hitting innocent bystanders. Although the first legally armed citizen was shot five times, he survived his wounds and was paralyzed due to a severely injured spine. In a radio interview, the legally armed citizen stated he still believes he did the right thing.

Another example of confronting an active shooter occurred on June

8, 2014, in a Wal-Mart in Las Vegas, Nevada. Two shooters (a husband and wife team) had just fled from a separate crime scene where they had ambushed and killed two uniformed police officers who were having lunch. When the male shooter entered the Wal-Mart, he fired into the ceiling and told patrons to get out. A legally armed citizen confronted the male shooter. The male shooter's accomplice (his wife) approached the legally armed citizen from his blind spot and killed him.

If you are going to use a firearm to stop an active shooter – don't verbally challenge him/her. When a person is on a murderous rampage and in the process of actively killing innocent people, I do not believe any law, in any jurisdiction, would require a person to first verbally warn the killer prior to using deadly force to stop them. Analysis of how legally armed citizens confronted the Tacoma Mall shooter and the Los Vegas Wal-Mart shooters illustrates their failure to use proper tactics, as well as the lack of a proper survivor mindset when going into an armed encounter. These failures are not intended to cast the legally armed citizens in a negative light, but their actions can teach us valuable lessons should we find ourselves in a similar situation.

Deciding Whether or Not to Engage the Shooter

There are several documented cases where an active shooter began a shooting rampage and legally armed citizens were present and armed at the time, but they elected not to engage the shooter. Most places that provide concealed weapons training do not address how to engage the active shooter, nor advocate doing so.

In the September 6, 2011, shooting in Carson City, Nevada, the gunman was using a fully automatic AK-47. Although there was a legally armed person inside the restaurant at the time of the shooting, he felt his weapon was no match for the fully automatic assault rifle and chose not to engage the gunman.

In another case, on December 11, 2012, at the Clackamas Mall just outside Portland, Oregon, a gunman wearing tactical clothing and a hockey mask entered the mall and started shooting at people with an assault rifle. The shooter killed two people and wounded another person. The gunman was working on his rifle and kept pulling the charging handle and hitting the side. With that break in the gunfire, one legally armed citizen pulled out his own gun but never fired it at the shooter. He thought that if he missed, he might accidentally shoot someone else. The legally armed citizen believes the gunman saw him and therefore used his last shot to end his life. The Clackamas Town Center had a posted policy of prohibiting firearms on the premises.

The decision not to engage the shooter may have been made for a variety of reasons:

- Firepower of the shooter. In at least one of the shootings, the assailant was armed with an assault rifle. The legally armed citizen was armed with a handgun and later stated that he felt that he could not match the firepower of the AK-47.
- Age of the shooter. In at least one of the shootings, the legally armed citizen approached the shooter, but upon noticing the shooter was significantly younger, verbally challenged the shooter and was shot by him.
- Unwillingness of the defender to use deadly force. In at least one of the shootings, the legally armed citizen could not bring himself to initiate and use deadly force against a shooter.

The decision to engage the shooter should be based on these factors:

- Circumstances of the event. The legally armed defender must quickly assess the situation and decide whether the odds are in their favor. Using surprise to launch a counterattack, the legally armed defender can use their firearm to efficiently incapacitate the active shooter.
- Willingness to use deadly force. The legally armed defender must know the applicable state laws that govern justifiable

homicide and the use of deadly force. The defender must, without doubt or hesitation, be capable of using that appropriate level of force to stop the active shooter.

- Firepower of defender. The firearm used by the legally armed defender must be of a sufficient caliber that it will stop the active shooter. The defender must be aware of shot placement when applying deadly force.

- Location of the defender's firearm. The defender must have the ability to draw and use the firearm with relative ease and safety when the threat is present. Having a weapon safely stowed inside a vehicle when the defender is away from the vehicle places the defender at a disadvantage. The defender would need to get to the vehicle, obtain the weapon, and return to the location where the shooting is occurring. This raises several issues regarding whether the defender is capable of escaping the kill zone and, if so, whether the defender will risk the danger of returning to the kill zone once they have effectively escaped. Statistically speaking, the time it takes for a defender to retrieve a weapon may be too long. The defender is at risk of being shot by responding law enforcement officers, who may interpret any person with a weapon as a threat. Additionally, the defender may not be able to escape the kill zone to obtain their weapon from another location. Therefore, the method and location in which the legally armed defender is carrying the firearm is a factor. If anyone elects to carry a weapon, the weapon needs to be concealed on the defender's person to have the greatest ability of deployment.

- Competence and confidence of the defender. If the shooter is wearing body armor, the rounds fired by the defender must be placed to strike the available and applicable targets. The legally armed defender must therefore have the ability, confidence, and willingness to make such shots reliably. The defender must also be competent in combat situations with their firearm. Shooting at stationary paper targets will be different from shooting at a person. Depending on the location of the shooting, the defender may need to engage the shooter from behind cover or while the defender is moving.

The Criminal Justice System

Most law enforcement agencies and legal systems operate under a system in which the only facts allowed in evidence to legally protect the armed citizen will be those that are pieced together and presented to law enforcement after the event is over. If the legally armed defender acts on information that cannot be fully supported by law enforcement after the event, the legally armed defender has placed themselves in legal jeopardy. Therefore, never assume anything. Do not engage anyone at gunpoint until you are 100 percent sure that you can do so legally, lawfully, and with relative safety. However, the bottom line is that you need to survive. In making the decision, you should think about whether you will be able to look into the mirror every day and truthfully say that you made the right decision either to engage or not to engage the shooter.

Priorities for the Legally Armed Defender

Take immediate cover and, only if the opportunity presents itself, draw your weapon and prepare the launch a surprise counterattack. The best time to do this is just before the shooter presents themselves to you. Your shots are designed to stop the killing of yourself and those around you, as well as to quickly incapacitate the shooter. The defender needs to understand that the shooter may be any age or gender. If the shooter is in the process of actively shooting and killing people, you can and should use deadly force against them. Not utilizing immediate and sufficient force to stop this threat places everyone present in further danger.

Never give an active shooter any advantage. Before an individual can act, they have to observe the hazard, consider ways to avoid the hazard, and then implement an avoidance strategy. Action is always faster than reaction. Imagine that you are holding someone at gunpoint and the other person is attempting to pull out a concealed weapon hidden behind his or her back and shoot you with it. You can only fire when you can see that the weapon has been drawn. In the time that it takes you to see that your opponent has drawn a weapon and decide to pull the trigger, the other person will likely already have shot you. The time it takes for you to perceive the threat and pull the trigger is longer than the time it takes for your opponent to act. At best, you will both pull the trigger simultaneously. With that in mind, why should any defender give the active shooter a time advantage?

In the case of the 1991 Luby's Cafeteria shooting and the 2005 Tacoma, Washington, mall shooting, laws had been put in place that prohibited law-abiding citizens from bringing firearms onto the property. I am not advocating that you violate any law. However, the active shooter will break many laws by bringing a weapon onto the property and shooting people. You must decide for yourself if you are prepared to be caught out by an active shooter without your firearm.

Never verbally confront an active shooter. Remember that the active shooter has entered a facility or area with the intent to shoot and kill innocent people. The shooter may have specific targets in mind, and in some cases, the shooter has elected to attack the desired targets only and may leave others alone. However, in other cases, the desired targets were unavailable for some reason and the shooter has chosen targets of opportunity, shooting anyone in sight. Attempting to verbally confront or negotiate with a shooter is never recommended. Remember, the shooter is often suicidal as well as homicidal. Why should a shooter who does not care about his or her own life care about yours? Some supposed authorities on the subject advocate using a loud voice to command the shooter. This tactic is never a good idea. This simply makes your presence known to the shooter, who may then target you for yelling. A loud voice will never match the lethal force of a firearm. Some people have assumed that because they know the shooter, the shooter would not be as inclined to shoot them. This is never an assumption you should make. Always consider your safety and those who love you and want to see you after that incident. This is no time for heroics or to use logic on an illogical and irrational person.

Never leave shelter to seek out an active shooter. Many jurisdictions allow for the average citizen to legally apply for, receive training in, and carry a concealed weapon. By carrying that concealed weapon, you need to give great consideration to what you would do if you find yourself in the vicinity of an active shooting. Without the training, experience, and proper mindset to engage in an armed confrontation, you are only putting yourself at greater risk.

During my police career, I have drawn my weapon on felony suspects who posed a potentially deadly threat to me and those around me. On each occasion, I had the benefit of police training and access to a range of tools. These tools included my primary and secondary firearms, a 12-guage shotgun, a semi-automatic AR-15 rifle, extra ammunition, and a police radio to communicate with other police personnel to call for assistance. I also had handcuffs to restrain the assailant, a bulletproof vest with a trauma shield, a bright flashlight for low light conditions, and the knowledge to track the assailant's movements from a place of cover. I had the benefit of being in a police uniform and in an obvious police car so that others within that immediate area could easily see that I was one of the good guys. My prior experiences in many armed confrontations as a law enforcement officer made me confident and prepared to act with a moment's notice. Anyone who willingly takes on an active shooter without the use of all of the above tools is placing themselves in a very precarious and dangerous situation.

As soon as the shooting starts, police will respond, and anyone seen or described as having a firearm will be deemed a threat. Police are trained to respond to deadly force by using equal or greater force. It may not be apparent to responding officers that you are not a threat to the safety of the community.

The shooter may also have access to and employ weapons that far outweigh and overmatch what you may legally possess. Taking on an armed assailant who has improvised explosive devices and is armed with fully automatic weapons with a small semi-automatic pistol is not a fair fight. Do not allow an unrealistic, misguided, or overwhelming sense of responsibility push you to place your life, or the lives of your friends and family, in grave danger.

Always assume that there is more than one active shooter. On June 8, 2014, in Las Vegas, Nevada, two shooters (a husband and wife) were fleeing from the shooting and entered a Wal-Mart. After entering the store, one of the two suspects fired shots in the air and told customers to leave. One legally-armed citizen decided to intervene and confronted the shooter, believing that he was alone. The female suspect approached the legally armed citizen and shot him.

Tactical Errors Made by Legally Armed Defenders

- *Failure to recognize and fully comprehend the complexities and deadly threat of an active shooter.* The shooter will unleash unprecedented violence upon any person present within the killing zone, regardless of age, gender, or status.
- *Failure to mentally rehearse the options and tactics they could use.* Prior to any event, the potential defender should mentally rehearse being in an active shooting. The defender should visualize a variety of tactics and scenarios, playing the "what if" game several times a month. This game will allow the defender to construct defenses to their best tactical advantage in advance of any real event. Therefore, when a real event does occur, the defender will have mentally rehearsed a multitude of scenarios and will be prepared to respond.
- *Failure to have a thorough understanding of the use of deadly force.* During an active shooter event, the shooter's actions and presence represent a deadly force threat. The potential

defender (being aware of the governing state law) should act accordingly. Most laws concerning the justifiable use of deadly force cover the defense of the person's life or the lives of others.

- *Assuming a law enforcement officer's role and attempting to take the assailant into custody.* During an active shooting, there is no responsibility for any citizen to take the assailant into custody. Attempting to do so could place the defender in danger. Taking any individual into custody is extremely difficult, especially in an armed and dangerous encounter, and takes training and resources that the defender does not have.

- *Failure to eradicate tunnel vision.* During a life-threatening event, it is not uncommon to develop tunnel vision. The defender focuses in on an extremely narrow view of the threat and is therefore unable to see all potential threats within the immediate area.

- *Not covering their backs.* When facing any threat to your personal safety, it is important to cover your back. You can have a known and trusted person watch your back for you, or you can place yourself in such a position that no one can get behind you.

- *Not shooting the assailant and instead engaging them in conversation.* Two cases (Oregon Mall, 2012, and the Las Vegas Wal-Mart, 2014) involve an active shooter being confronted by a legally armed citizen. In both cases, the assailant was not shot and the legally armed citizen was met by gunfire from either the assailant or the assailant's accomplice.

- *Failure to understand that an active shooter may have one or more accomplices (males and females).* In the Las Vegas Wal-Mart case, the wife of the shooter accompanied her husband from one crime scene to the next. Although not as common, females have been active shooters and should not be dismissed when assessing potential threats.

- *Being influenced or swayed by the youth of the shooter to not respond with deadly force.* Past active shooters have been youths that attended a particular school and have killed students and teachers. The shooter is homicidal, and it is never recommended to not meet deadly force with equal force.

- *Failure to understand the perception-reaction concept.* Action is always faster than reaction. You must first see the threat, comprehend what is occurring, decide what to do, and then react by implementing an action of your own.

- *Deciding to confront or warn the shooter before taking action.* In western movies, the good guy always warns the bad guy before taking action, and that bad guy can only be met in a face-to-face confrontation. However, in real-life situations, these tactics should not be employed. Confronting the shooter does not make you look like the good guy. In reality, it makes you the dead guy. The weapon you chose to legally conceal should also be of sufficient caliber to incapacitate the shooter with minimal rounds and should be optimized for concealed carry. Firing warning shots in an attempt to discourage the active shooter from violent actions is never recommended.

Notifying Law Enforcement of a Shooting

If you have the time, you may be able use a cell phone to contact law enforcement prior to engaging the armed assailant. If a spouse, significant other, or friend is making the call for you, ensure that the caller relays the following information:

- Shots fired
- Location of the shooting
- The type of weapon the shooter is using (if known)
- Suspect's physical description (if known)
- Your exact location
- Your identity, physical description, and clothing description
- The type of weapon you have
- Why it is that waiting for law enforcement is not an option

Once law enforcement enters the area, they will engage the active shooter using deadly force. If you are going to engage the shooter with your legally-owned weapon, never count on law enforcement to know that you are the good guy and not the bad guy, and to therefore hold their fire. In these situations, your life is in danger from two different threats: the shooter and the responding police. Therefore, if you elect to use deadly force against an active shooter, draw your weapon and incapacitate the shooter only when the shooter presents themselves to you. Then immediately holster your weapon, stay behind cover, and wait for the arrival of law enforcement. Do not approach the injured shooter. You are not required to take the shooter into custody or render first aid. Wait for law enforcement to arrive, and make sure there is nothing in your hands that remotely resembles a weapon. You will need to advise responding officers that you are armed and engaged the assailant in gunfire. Remember that these officers will not know you are the good guy and may treat you as a suspect until they know otherwise. The protocols that police may follow during their initial investigation may not make you feel comfortable, but it's what they need to do to ensure their safety and the safety of others around them.

On February 12, 2007, at the Trolley Square Mall located in Salt Lake City, Utah, a gunman entered the mall, shot five people dead, and wounded at least four others. The shooter was armed with a shotgun with a pistol grip, a handgun, and a backpack full of ammunition. An off-duty plainclothes police officer was just leaving a restaurant with his wife, who was a police dispatcher, when they heard popping sounds. After several more popping sounds, he looked over the second floor railing to see numerous injured people on the ground. The shooter was spotted walking out of a store armed with a shotgun. The off-duty officer yelled to the people around him on the second floor that he was an off-duty officer and that they should get down. With his gun drawn and grabbing his off-duty ID, he continued to shout to identify himself as an officer. Due to the off-duty officer yelling, the shooter spotted him and fired. The officer told his wife to call 911, and she relayed that her husband was an off-duty officer, not a second gunman, and that he was actively engaging the suspect. She also described her husband's physical appearance and the clothing he was wearing. A responding officer (unknown to the off-duty officer) arrived, and it took a moment for the responding officer to assess the situation, although the off-duty officer was continuously yelling that he was an officer. The off-duty officer later said that he was briefly worried that he could be misidentified as the shooter due to his civilian clothes. Due to the investigation, the off-duty officer cannot disclose how many rounds he fired, but he did share that his limited cache of ammo was a point of concern. Shortly afterward, the off-duty officer heard the sound of automatic and semi-automatic gunfire, an indication that SWAT teams had arrived inside the building and were engaging the shooter. The suspect was successfully engaged and neutralized. The entire episode only lasted approximately three minutes, in which time five people were murdered (two men, two women, and a fifteen-year-old girl) and four others were critically wounded. This off-duty officer's story has inspired other police officers to carry their service weapons off-duty, even after years of going unarmed. The off-duty officer has said that he feels he would've been another victim if he had not been armed.

Lockdown

If you find yourself in a lockdown environment with a shooter outside of your area, stay where you are until the lockdown has been lifted or wait until law enforcement arrives and actually evacuates your area. However, if your situation drastically deteriorates and your life is in immediate jeopardy, you may be forced to make a tactical evacuation using a route in which the shooter is not likely to be present.

If you have locked down inside a familiar environment (such as your work or school), the lockdown and "all clear" procedures may have been explained. If not, how will you know when the "all clear" has been announced? In some locations, that information may be communicated via e-mail. In other locations, an announcement may be made over the public address system. Law enforcement may evacuate citizens by accessing the locked area with a key obtained by a responsible official from that particular facility. Do not open any locked doors when prompted by a voice from outside the door. A worst case scenario is to unlock the door when prompted by such a voice, only to discover the shooter is the one who posed as an evacuating agency.

If you are in doubt as to whether the "all clear" status has been announced, do not unlock your door or leave your area. You may call the emergency communications center directly to confirm the "all clear" status. Advise the center that you have been in a lockdown environment and request instructions. If law enforcement officers have not located you during their search of the facility, they may prefer you remain in that area or they may ask you to exit the area alone. Consider that things may still be a little unstable and use extreme caution when moving. Remain as calm as possible, and follow all instructions of the law enforcement officers.

In the event that law enforcement officers need to evacuate you from a very unstable environment, they will have many issues to attend to, such as protecting the group from any threats while also assessing the group being rescued for any suspicious activity. Try not to add any extra responsibilities, and don't ask questions or make demands. It is best to follow instructions and safely leave the area. Once you are outside the immediate area, law enforcement may detain you until they have determined that you are not a suspect and have gathered crucial information for their subsequent investigation. Please provide law enforcement all the assistance they require.

If you are in a once-safe area that is in the process of being breached by the shooter and you feel compelled to escape to save your life, this is when having an escape route and plan from the place where you are sheltering can be extremely valuable. Consider either making a tactical evacuation from your sheltered location or physically and violently confronting the shooter. Your choice of evacuation or confrontation may be contingent on your physical ability and comfort level. Keep in mind that, while you are evacuating, you may be suddenly and unexpectedly confronted by the shooter. Be prepared to take physical lifesaving action at any point during your escape.

If you are legally armed, leaving the safe area to search for the shooter is never a good idea and places you and those who may be with you in grave mortal danger. Leave the safe area only when you know that it is no longer safe to remain due to the shooter's direct actions. Also, ensure that when you are being rescued by law enforcement, you do not have a weapon of any kind in your hands. If you have a concealed weapon on your person, advise law enforcement that you have a weapon you are carrying legally so they make take the proper precautions to ensure everyone's safety.

After the Shooting

When law enforcement arrives on the scene and discover an individual who has discharged a firearm, they will need to ensure citizen and officer safety. The person who did the shooting will be detained. This detention is to determine that the shooting was a lawful or justified shooting that falls within the parameters of the law. The person—in this case, the legally armed citizen who fired a weapon to stop the active shooter—will be processed as a potential suspect and evidence will be collected.

It is probable that your adrenalin will be elevated after having survived an encounter with an active shooter, and you may be in shock. It is recommended that you seek legal counsel. This does not reflect any wrongdoing on the account of the law enforcement officers, but rather is to ensure that the extensive protocol and custodial interrogation does not evoke excited statements from you that could prove damaging in subsequent criminal and/or civil trial. You should not make any written statements without first consulting an attorney. If you are legally armed and intend to carry your firearm in public, I highly recommend that you contact a criminal defense attorney in advance. This is not because you expect to commit a crime, but rather that in the unlikely event that you need to use your firearm to save your life, you want to have the details of a competent attorney that you can trust to protect your rights.

For evidence collection, all weapons fired or used by the defender will be collected and processed. It is unlikely that you will ever regain possession of this weapon, as it may be used in subsequent criminal and civil proceeding. As the defender, you will probably be tested for gunshot residue to confirm that you fired a weapon. You may have photographs taken of you to provide a record of your physical appearance at the time of the shooting. There may be trace evidence on your clothing that will be collected by forensics. You may also be required to submit to drug and alcohol testing. With that in mind, it is not advisable to drink to excess in a public place. Should a shooting occur and you take action, your level of intoxication will become a factor, both in your survival and in subsequent legal proceedings.

Additional Dangers

In a terrorist attack, it is common for the attackers to launch a secondary attack designed to kill additional victims in combination with the initial attack. For this reason, take great care at the scene of any active shooting or large-scale attack.

Consider that a secondary shooter or explosive device may be planted along escape routes. Beware of any place where large numbers of people may gather after a shooting or bombing event. When any violent attack occurs, people will typically gather near the location. Some of them will be victims who have been evacuated and have chosen to stay around and see what is happening. They may also be in mild to moderate shock and may not fully comprehend the situation. Make sure that you move a significant distance away from the area in case there are any additional attacks.

For those who feel compelled to arrive at the scene, possibly to look or wait for loved ones, be careful not to become another victim. Usually, law enforcement will designate a safe location where they prefer onlookers to wait until the scene is rendered safe and they can reunite with loved ones. Such areas should be cleared by law enforcement officers prior to potential victims or witnesses being sequestered within that area. Until the area has been cleared, stay away from trash containers, backpacks, or vehicles. Overall, resist the urge to stand around and watch. This is never a good idea at the scene of a mass casualty event. Until law enforcement has investigated, even supposed accidents may be more dangerous than they appear. As a curious onlooker, you are simply another potential casualty that emergency services have to take care of, and your presence can get in the way of them helping those most in need and securing the area against further attack. What is a safe distance? You might be safe at least three large city blocks away from the scene. That is a good distance to wait for events to unfold or for news on the condition of a loved one.

Avoid areas where a critical incident has occurred or is occurring. Identify a local news source that would broadcast live in the case of an active shooting or mass casualty event in your area. When you become aware of such an event, tune in for regular updates. If you are traveling in that direction, try to avoid the entire area. Consider suspending travel altogether if you are unable to give the location an extremely wide margin.

Being in the midst of the chaos will only complicate issues for those who are already present, and it may also place you in danger. Being nearby or travelling in the direction of the event will hamper emergency responders who will be trying to access the site long after the initial units have arrived. If you need to enter the area to pick up someone who has been stranded, remember that cell phone coverage may be temporarily interrupted or blocked. Text can therefore be the most efficient way of contacting people. Keep in mind that in cases of gang shootings, the attackers may know which hospital has received the victims and so may choose to continue their attack in the hospital. Be prepared to evacuate or shelter in place at the hospital in the unlikely event that a shooting occurs there.

Aftermath

After any shooting, the affected area is designated a crime scene. Depending on the number of victims, the notoriety of the event, and other related factors, the crime scene may be enlarged. Personal belongings within that area may be unreachable. Access to businesses, residences, and vehicles may not be possible. Forensic investigators will need to take their time as they process the crime scene and collect valuable evidence. Witnesses to all aspects of the event will need to be interviewed to allow law enforcement to understand all aspects of the incident, from its inception to the final resolution. Video surveillance is an important tool in supporting witness statements, as their views may be skewed due to emotional trauma.

Remember that being involved in an active shooting has nothing to do with you as a person. Do not allow the event to define who you are or how you live the remainder of your life. No matter the context, you have suffered a traumatic, life-threatening event and survived. This last fact is the most important. This is the time to reclaim who you are and what you mean to your friends and family. This is a time to reconnect with everyone in your life who truly loves you. Surround yourself with positive people who can provide you with the support you need.

Understanding PTSD

All direct participants (and even some indirect participants) of an active shooting may possibly exhibit signs of post-traumatic stress disorder (PTSD) and should understand some of the symptoms and seek immediate professional assistance if necessary. PTSD is not a sign of weakness, but failure to act to address any potential psychological issues can be harmful to traumatized individuals, as well as their loved ones, who may feel useless and unable to help. Some signs of PTSD include the following:

- *Alcohol or drug problems:* Using drugs or alcohol might be harming your health and relationships. It could be a sign of substance abuse or dependence.
- *Trouble sleeping:* Sleep problems can interfere with relationships, work, physical health, and the ability to get through the day.
- *Relationship problems:* Relationship problems can make it difficult to enjoy life, both for you and your loved ones.
- *Feeling on edge:* Hypervigilance (feeling like you're constantly on guard) is a common response to a frightening, traumatic, or life-threatening experience. It doesn't have to interfere with your relationships, work, physical health, or ability to get through the day.
- *Social withdrawal/isolation:* Finding that you prefer or seek out a social withdrawal and isolation that can make it hard to enjoy life or relate to other people.
- *Fear of specific locations:* The area where the shooting event took place (workplace, school, the mall) or similar types of places may be a source of fear and impede your daily activities.

Physical activities, such as yoga, running, or other exercise, can help with your mental health. Seek counsel from a mental health professional or spiritual advisor. From personal experience, I can attest to the importance of seeking professional help in dealing with issues related to such a traumatic event. No one expects you to be unaffected by such needless death and destruction. While life offers many positive experiences, after such an event, it is normal and helpful to seek help in guiding yourself back onto a more productive and fulfilling path.

Part 5
Strategic Defense Recommendations

· ·

Whether you are a school administrator, business executive, middle manager, line supervisor, employee, or just the average person, employing one or more of these strategies may help to prevent or mitigate the effects of an active shooter. In this section, you will find specific and general recommendations for certain industries, businesses, or leisure locations. Please read the strategy for schools before going further and, if those sections apply for your particular industry, don't be shy about applying any tactic. The goal is to make it extremely difficult or almost impossible for the active shooter or other armed assailant to be successful in an attack at any location.

Schools

Safety is the top priority for all individuals within a school environment and should be the primary concern for every school administrator. If students are incapable of being secure in their classrooms and on the school grounds, resources and training should immediately be used to remedy the situation.

Structural measures are an important starting point. Access control, target hardening of doors, bulletproof glass (especially at the front entrances and throughout the school), fencing the property, video surveillance, and CCTV are all good ideas for averting an externally based shooter. Several older elementary schools have classrooms that are linked to one another and to the bathroom with doors, rather than through a hallway. These schools should install deadbolt locks and/or cypher locks on doors. In other areas, a double cylinder deadbolt that uses a key (not a thumb turn) could be used.

Doors, windows, classroom walls, and administrative areas should be refurbished to protect sheltering individuals. If teachers and students are going to be forced to shelter and hide inside a classroom, the classroom needs to be refurbished to facilitate that need. All classroom doors should open from the interior of the classroom in an outward direction. This construction prevents a door from being forced inward by an intruder. Installing a bullet-resistant steel plate within the door prevents bullets being fired through the door into the classroom. Classroom walls could also be fortified in the same way to prevent shots being fired into a classroom from outside. All windows should be replaced with bullet-resistant glass, and interior windows should potentially be reconfigured to be more secure. In administrative areas, a safe room/place should be constructed so that administrative personnel can shelter in place if necessary. Communication during an event is vital to the survival of those involved in the emergency, and communication systems need to be in place in any location where students or staff may shelter. Ensure that the teacher's desk in each classroom is not across the room and directly in line with the door by wiring the computer cables to facilitate that purpose, rather than allow the desk to be placed where the computer wiring is convenient. In many older buildings, cell phone reception is not reliable, and this can hamper rescue attempts by law enforcement. Reception throughout the school should be mapped, and any dead spots should be remedied.

School administrators need to consider that threats can come from their own ranks, including students, former students, faculty and their spouses. Unlike these internally based threats, who have especially easy access to the interior, externally based threats have typically begun their attack from the exterior of the school and have attempted to breach the interior of the school to continue their carnage. These shooters have approached the front door of the school (Newtown, Connecticut) or have approached via the playground (Stockton, California).

On December 14, 2012, in Newtown, Connecticut, a twenty-year-old suspect fatally shot twenty children and six adult staff members. The suspect shot and killed his mother at their Newtown home prior to the school shootings. As first responders arrived, the suspect committed suicide. In Stockton, California, on January 17, 1989, an anonymous person telephoned the Stockton Police Department regarding a death threat against Cleveland Elementary School. At noon that day, a disturbed drifter and former Stockton resident began his attack by setting his van on fire. The shooter used a Molotov cocktail after parking the van behind the school, causing the van to explode. He then moved to the school playground and began firing from behind a portable building. The suspect fired 106 rounds in three minutes, killing five children and wounding thirty others, including one teacher. All of the fatally shot victims and many of the wounded were Cambodian and Vietnamese immigrants. The shooter then committed suicide.

School districts and private schools should realize that once these items have been implemented, more action is required to protect the school from both internally and externally based threats. Remember, target-hardening alone will not prove effective for any internally based shooter, who is already a current student or school employee. In those cases, the student already has access to the school. Those physical and structural measures alone are not sufficient.

Ensure that someone is always on duty and actively looking for threats. School shootings have occurred at a variety of times throughout the day, from just before the start of school to the end of the school day. Duty assignments for teachers at the beginning of school, during recess, over lunch, and at the end of the day are vital. It should not be possible for any potential shooter to approach the school via any entrance without being first observed by personnel. Unfortunately, school personnel who are out on the school grounds are often ill-prepared for any emergency due to the lack of communication equipment, lack of education, and persistence of traditional response strategies. School personnel need to be alert to violent events that could occur from within the confines of their school. Each and every duty person needs to have the necessary equipment to communicate a threat when one is perceived. Equipping teachers with radios is only the start. The duty personnel need to know what to look for and what to do should the situation unfold in front of them.

During the 2013 shooting that occurred in the middle school in Sparks, Nevada, there was a schoolteacher on duty at the time. The male teacher heard the gunshot and, with radio in hand, approached the shooter—a current student. As the teacher approached, he verbally addressed the student, who had already fired at least one shot. The student raised his semi-automatic pistol, killed the teacher, and then shot himself.

Teachers and school administrators who are on duty need to remember that they are responsible for safeguarding the people inside. Just because there have never been any shooting incidents at the school before, this does not mean that duty personnel can be complacent. It only takes a few seconds to realize that someone is a threat and to act appropriately.

Appropriate surveillance and flexibility are important for surviving an active shooting. Should a shooting event occur in which the interior of the school is too unsafe to use as a safe place, shelter should be sought elsewhere. Although the Sparks Middle School shooting occurred outside the building, school children and parents who were outside chose to move into the neighborhood to seek shelter rather than attempt to enter the school. Be flexible enough to adjust your safety plan accordingly, as your life just may depend on that flexibility. The use of video surveillance and CCTV can be extremely helpful for school personnel and responding law enforcement officers, as the images can be viewed at the school and elsewhere. For example, a school captures the image of an attack occurring. The office staff (viewing locally) or law enforcement (viewing remotely) can see the assailant as the attack progresses throughout the school and can alert those concerned about the assailant's location and direction of travel. They can also alert staff about the location of students or staff who need immediate medical assistance or who need to be directed to shelter. Some teachers and staff are instructed that once their doors are locked during a code red, they are not to open their classroom doors to anyone, as they cannot be certain that a student attempting to gain entrance is not a threat. Video surveillance allows staff to remotely monitor students caught in the hallways and instruct the nearest classroom teacher to admit them.

Ensure that each classroom is prepared for extended lockdown. In most active shootings, the lockdown can easily become hours. Students may become hungry. Teachers can easily store snacks for such emergencies, and cheap items with a long shelf life are preferable. Students may also need to use the restroom. A portable bathroom within the classroom may be valuable.

Ensure that teachers and staff receive appropriate training. With the unfortunate increase in the frequency and death toll of school shootings, tactical disarming techniques should be taught to every school employee. This training should take place at least twice a year. Making attendance mandatory ensures that the real victims are educated and empowered to participate in saving their own lives, should the need arise. Additionally, each person needs to understand their role in the event of a shooting, and the roles of all other employees within the school, so that each person knows what they are expected to do and what they can expect others to do. Training should include the best and worst case scenarios, as well as a contingency plan for if the shooter has breached the teacher's location and the teacher needs to physically defend themselves against a violent attack. Active shooter defense training should be comprehensive, and it should be mandatory for every teacher, substitute teacher, and school official to have completed this training before their first day. Employees should not be instructed to attempt to talk with an active shooter, no matter the shooter's age or apparent vulnerability. In the majority of cases, this has resulted in the shooter targeting the individual who is talking.

Fire drills are a particularly vulnerable time for a school in terms of the safety of the students and staff. Most schools have a mandated number of fire drills they need to perform within a specific time. The most common reaction to a fire drill is for students and staff to exit the closest exterior door and line up on school grounds with their fellow classmates while their teachers take attendance. These fire drills should be coordinated with the school police to ensure sufficient resources are present during the fire drill, specifically to observe and deter any individual who might use this time to launch an attack. In the event of an actual fire alarm, school police should always respond to protect the evacuated students, in addition to the fire department. Special care should be taken at this time, especially if there is no apparent fire within the school.

On March 24, 1998, two young boys (thirteen and eleven years old) shot several of their classmates in Jonesboro, Arkansas. The younger of the two boys asked to be excused from class, pulled the school fire alarm, and then ran to join the older boy, who was already in a wooded area. As the students exited the school, the two boys began shooting. Four students and one teacher were killed, and ten other students were wounded. The two boys were caught, and in their possession were thirteen fully loaded firearms, including three semi-automatic rifles, and 200 rounds of ammunition.

Ensure that escape routes are available. Due to the current philosophy of the single point of entry, all the gates and doors of a school are locked with padlocks, thus preventing anyone from truly using that avenue of escape should a deadly encounter develop. This is problematic if a shooting occurs inside the school while staff and students are outside, as they will be unable to enter the school from the back and seek shelter. These padlocks should all be keyed the same, and all school employees should have a key in case an evacuation from that area is required. Additionally, if a group is caught outside when shots are fired and escape is possible, they should leave the school grounds and go into the neighborhood, if that is the safest tactic.

When I broached this possibility with some school administrators, they commented that the school district would never sanction leaving the school grounds to seek safety and/or shelter elsewhere. Several months later, that same school district had an active shooting where the shooting took place outside the school before class began. All exterior doors to the back of the school were locked down for their single point of entry policy. Students and parents elected to leave the confines of the school grounds and seek safety and shelter within the neighborhood.

Remember to treat an active shooter inside the school as if the building was on fire. All those who are able should leave the immediate area and seek safety and shelter elsewhere. If staff and students are outside the school and the shooter is inside the school, they should not run into the building or instruct others to do so.

Create a distinctive warning system for an active shooting/code red. This should be a separate and distinct audible alarm that cannot be mistaken for the school fire alarm. This alarm should provide an audible signal instead of relying on e-mails, texts, or PA systems to notify staff. These techniques can still be utilized, but only after the audible alarm has been activated. The alarm notifies everyone on the property at the same time and gives them an opportunity to escape the area or seek better shelter. This particular alarm could also be monitored so that immediate response from law enforcement would be initiated.

Invest in neighborhood safety. Local school administration, along with local law enforcement, should work with neighbors adjacent to the school to identify safe houses. Care should be taken to identify sex offenders and possible predators who may reside within those areas. Possible locations along popular walking routes could be identified by staff and parents, and these could then be communicated to police to ascertain whether these locations are truly safe. Parents who are able to walk their children to school should do so. Not only is this a great bonding and exercise opportunity, but it also helps safeguard children during this period. Not all parents need to walk their children to school, though, and walking patrols (much like carpooling) could be organized through the school. Each parent doing so needs appropriate attire for the weather and a working cell phone for emergencies.

Enlist threat management professionals to perform an independent site survey and determine the vulnerability of the school. This should be done by an outside entity that has no specific agenda in mind. Employing outside professional vendors allows fresh eyes to look at the problem areas for each school building and to make objective observations and recommendations. This also prevents the possibility of becoming too complacent.

Create a threat assessment team for the school or school district. This team would be comprised of mental health professionals, school police, teachers, and administrators. Any student who is thought to be a potential threat should be referred to the team. A decision and course of action should be recommended for each student that comes to the attention of the team. The course of action needs to include a plan of action, whether it is suspension or expulsion from school, mental health care, or intervention of the juvenile or adult criminal justice system. Keep in mind that in some cases, shooting cases have occurred when an individual has fallen through the cracks and proper follow-up care failed to occur. Periodic reassessments are necessary to ensure that the measures are effective.

The school should have a policy that requires mandatory documentation and action on all legitimate threatening behaviors. In many cases, it emerges afterward that the organization knew about the potential threat but did not act appropriately or in time. Those responsible should be held accountable for this lack of communication, whether it is due to a lack of documentation, administrative laziness, misguided policies, or a lack of direction as to whose responsibility it was to take action. Documentation of threatening behavior and violent acts needs to accurately reflect the factual events of the incident. You should not attempt to whitewash the incident or downplay it, as this does not allow those responsible to accurately assess the nature of the threat or how best to respond. When officials need to take administrative actions against a violent or potentially violent person (student or staff member), it is crucial that they have written access to the facts. Common sense should be used in this assessment, and professionals can be used to provide an objective and sensible pair of eyes. It is important to distinguish between clocks for science class and bombs, and to distinguish between a gun formed from a piece of bread and a legitimately threatening action.

A student who has shown a demonstrated propensity for violence or who has committed significant violent acts does not belong in a school with innocent children. Those types of students need to be removed immediately and not allowed anywhere near the campus. Using today's technology, those types of students can continue their education by registering online or by homeschooling until such time as they are no longer a threat to themselves or others. This is a matter of public safety, not student privacy, and law and policy-makers need to ensure that when a student with a violent past wishes to transfer, the receiving school is aware of their record.

One student with a violent past transferred to a school in which only certain administrators knew of his record. They refused to warn teachers or other staff members about the student's past behavior. After several scary verbal confrontations with the student, staff inquired about the student's record at their previous school. Only then were they informed about his previous actions. The safety of the students and staff was jeopardized because someone felt that the student's privacy might be violated.

Provide trauma and emergency first aid training for school employees. In the event of an active shooting or mass casualty event, it can take hours before medical personnel are able to enter the building and treat the victims. Training employees in how to apply lifesaving first aid under those conditions may be a matter of life and death for those who have been severely injured. This training should be combined with the presence of fully stocked first aid kits in convenient locations throughout the school and in every classroom.

Take extra precautions for special events. Events such as athletic competitions and dances bring members of the general public into the school. For these types of events, school police need to be extremely vigilant in observing all attendees. Additional police resources should be present and focused on recognizing potential threats. They should also have a contingency plan in place should things go awry during the event.

Armed school police officers should be present at every school. These officers need to be properly trained, equipped, and staffed so that they are capable of addressing an active shooter. These personnel should be focused on preventing any violent attacks, rather than policing normal student violations. While this is an expensive proposition, schools spend larger sums on more frivolous outlays, such as retreats and speaking fees. Each officer needs to be properly equipped, just like a regular police officer. In addition, officers should have at their immediate disposal a long gun (such as an AR-15) and a Taser. Officers should train with the local police department to ensure that all law enforcement personnel are following the same procedures when responding to deadly force threats. Officers should undergo periodic training to include behavior detection as well as range training for the handgun, long gun, and Taser. Be sure to include all agencies who would potentially respond to a violent event in these practical exercises. Ensure that command personnel also meet on a regular basis to discuss the issues specific to their areas of responsibility and to ensure management will not hinder any rescue operations.

It is crucial that those responsible for school safety remain vigilant while on the premises. Violent episodes don't occur every day, and for that reason, it is extremely easy for complacency to set in. Do not allow complacency and social networking to interfere with the major task at hand: ensuring the safety of everyone on site. Make sure that you are 100 percent focused throughout the entirety of your shift, as lives depend on it.

Private/Public Businesses

This category affects all private and public businesses that may be considered soft targets, due to the lack of a visible and/or armed security detail. Such locations are typically movie theaters, shopping malls, hospitals, rehabilitation facilities, office buildings, airport baggage areas and government buildings at all levels that either do not have armed security, law enforcement or limited presence of those protection/deterents. Potential shooters may be attracted to these particular locations due to the minimal armed resistance, the notoriety that such a shooting may get them (like at government facilities), or the number of potential victims. Regardless of whether you are inside a building as an employee or customer, pay attention to people entering the facility that may have violent intentions. Be prepared to implement your personal survival plan at any location should you have evidence that a shooting may be about to take place or is occurring.

Places where large numbers of people congregate could attract an externally based shooter. Staff need to be trained and have emergency contingency plans already in place should they encounter an active shooter. Each facility has a moral (and often legal) obligation to take reasonable steps to safeguard its employees and the people who frequent their business. Reasonable steps for private and public businesses are similar to those for schools:

Access control, target hardenings, bullet-resistant glass at the front entrances, video surveillance, and CCTV. Realize that doing this alone will not stop, deter, or totally mitigate the threat of an active shooter. Therefore, spending thousands of dollars or resources in fortifying the entrances is not the sole answer, and a multifaceted response is necessary.

Use Uniformed and covert armed security/law enforcement personnel in public areas where large crowds of people may regularly assemble. Recently, shooters have exploited soft targets such as airport baggage claim and other less secure areas due to security being focused more on protection of the actual aircraft. Because of that focus, other areas have been exploited by shooter in Istanbul, Turkey and on January 6, 2017 at the Ft. Lauderdale, Florida airport. All security/law enforcement personnel (whether overtly or covertly assigned to those areas) need to have a viable means of instant identification/recognition to responding armed personnel to avoid friendly fire incidents. Use of raid jackets and emergency (Don't shoot me) banners provide instant identification to responding armed personnel and should provide a measure of safety for those armed personnel who may directly engage the shooter.

Provide realistic active shooter training for all facility personnel. When an active shooting event occurs, a significant number of people will look to facility staff for direction. When new employees are hired, it should be mandated they attend the training as part of their orientation. Each employee should know what they need to do when shots are fired.

Use a separate and distinct audible alarm for the active shooter. This should sound totally different from a fire alarm. This alarm would provide an audible signal so that everyone on the property is notified at the same time and has an opportunity to escape the area or seek better shelter. This should be monitored by law enforcement so that they can respond immediately. All members of your facility need to recognize that sound and be able implement their contingency plan upon hearing it. With workers who work behind closed doors, all audible alarms should be capable of being heard through closed doors, and red rotating lights should be visible in all areas.

Enlist threat management professionals to perform a site survey and threat vulnerability assessment. This should be done by an outside entity that has no politically influenced agenda in mind other than the safety of the facility and the people within that facility. Employing outside professional vendors allows fresh eyes to look at the problem areas and make objective observations of all threats. This also prevents the possibility of complacency and local organizational politics.

Ensure that cell phone reception is available throughout the building. Ensure that cell phone reception is available in any place in which individuals may shelter during an emergency. The ability to communicate is vital during any active shooting, and poor reception can hinder emergency services and law enforcement.

Ensure sound administrative policies and procedures are in place to protect employees and promote safety. Such policies will allow people to report threatening behavior and know that bullying tactics that can breed resentment are dealt with swiftly and in an appropriate manner. In addition, you need to establish clear consequences for filing fraudulent claims. Accusing another employee of misconduct that is fabricated is an offense that should never be tolerated.

Enforce mandatory documentation and action on all legitimate threatening behaviors. Documentation of threatening behavior and violent acts needs to accurately reflect the actual events. You should never downplay the incident, as this does not allow those responsible to accurately assess the nature of the threat or how best to respond. When officials need to take administrative actions against a violent or potentially violent person, it is crucial that they have written access to the facts. Any employee who has shown a demonstrated propensity for violence or who has committed violent acts against another employee does not belong in the workplace.

Create a threat assessment team for the facility. This will help identify internally based threats where the potential shooter is an employee. The team should be comprised of human resource professionals, facility leaders/administrators, and employee representatives. Any employee who is deemed a potential threat should be referred to this team for an assessment and appropriate action. The course of action needs to include a plan of action, which may include suspension, mandatory mental health evaluation and treatment before the employee returns to work, termination, or intervention by the criminal justice system. Periodic reassessments are necessary to ensure that the measures are effective.

Provide trauma and emergency first aid training for supervisors, managers, and designated employees. In the event of an active shooting or mass casualty event, it can take hours before medical personnel are able to enter the building and treat the victims. Remember that medical personnel will not usually be able to enter an area until it has been cleared by law enforcement. Depending on the size and complexity of the property, this could take some time. Training employees in how to apply lifesaving first aid under those conditions may be a matter of life and death for those who have been severely injured. These designated employees would initiate emergency first aid lifesaving measures with the intent of keeping individuals stable until relieved by competent medical personnel. This training should be combined with the presence of fully stocked first aid kits in convenient locations throughout the facility.

If necessary, ensure that your business has a plan for how to stay open while the crime scene is processed. Whenever a shooting occurs, especially if there are fatalities, law enforcement will close the affected areas to conduct rescue operations and investigate the crime scene. The entire process will be very lengthy, and areas will be closed off, possibly for several weeks. If it is essential that the business remain open, such as a hospital or government building, be prepared to move to an alternate worksite and conduct your business from there until your primary worksite is opened.

Train supervisors and managers to be conscientious and respectful, not just taskmasters. Although productivity is important, all employees need to be treated with dignity and respect. If your company does not already have one, construct and regularly review your policies on workplace violence and sexual harassment. These policies need to define workplace violence and sexual harassment, including all verbal and nonverbal acts, as well as the consequences for violating the policy. This policy must also instruct all employees to cooperate fully and truthfully with all administrative inquires and investigations. The policies should give clear consequences for employees who fail to fully cooperate or who give incomplete or false statements during the course of the inquiry or investigation. These types of administrative policies are mandatory to adequately deal with matters involving workplace violence, sexual harassment, and other potentially threatening behaviors.

Create risk managers and emergency managers who are focused on understanding and mitigating the threat of an active shooter. Some management officials do not know, or even want to know, all the details of the active shooter threat. By creating these key positions and ensuring that the managers fully grasp the scope of the active shooter threat and are focused on addressing that threat, employees have a higher chance of preventing or surviving a shooting event. These managers need to be an integral part of all public and private organizations. Emergency managers can get involved with professional networks and draw on the experiences of other companies that have faced mass casualty events in their locations. By combining their expertise, emergency managers are able to address a wide range of issues, including prevention, mitigation, and dealing with the aftermath of an event. Your risk manager and emergency manager should use the proven principles from the incident command systems (ICS), which have been used in other mass casualty events. The various components of the ICS will involve all functions of local, state, and sometimes federal government. These various functions have worked together many times on a host of real world natural disasters (floods, fires, tornados, earthquakes).

A more progressive emergency manager and risk manager will conduct tabletop and practical exercises with all emergency responders and stakeholders. Risk managers will be able to reach out to industry professionals to conduct a site survey for each public location. No matter the location or type of business, from city hall to the parks department and everywhere in between, if the public has access to it, that location should have a survey to ascertain its unique vulnerabilities. Once the survey reveals particular vulnerabilities, those areas can receive the necessary attention to secure them against a potential active shooting. Resist the urge to just employ easy fixes.

Private Security Professionals

People visiting your facility will look to security staff, as well as other employees, to direct them in an emergency. If facility security has not been appropriately educated on how to effectively safeguard your employees and customers, you could be liable in civil court. When it comes to the safety of your facility and of the people within it, you should leave no stone unturned and provide a range of tactical and practical survival techniques for every conceivable situation. Training should include the worst case scenario, where the shooter has forced their way into a location and your employees have to physically defend themselves. Not only will this help ensure the safety of your employees, but you will be more likely to survive the civil lawsuits that often come on the heels of an active shooting.

Tactical firearm disarming techniques should be taught to all supervisors, managers, and other key individuals. This type of training will empower the participants and provide lifesaving techniques should the need arise. It should occur at least twice a year and be either taught by or facilitated by private security professionals. Take into account the turnover of a particular business and ensure that this training is done as part of the standard employee orientation.

Create safe rooms within the business for employees and/or patrons. Safe rooms may need to be refurbished to facilitate sheltering in place and emergency communication with authorities. All safe room doors should open from the interior of the room in an outward direction— this is important, as it prevents a door from being forced inward by an intruder. Installing bullet-resistant plates within the door and walls will stop bullets being fired through them, injuring the occupants of the safe room.

If state law allows, consider designating trusted and trained individuals to carry concealed firearms on the premises. These chosen individuals should have been approved by local law enforcement and should be protected by company policy in the unlikely event they may have to deploy those weapons during an active shooting. The identities of these armed individuals can be concealed from all employees other than a small number of top managers. This will prevent the covertly armed individual from becoming a target for any active shooter. In the past, armed security officers have been specifically targeted by active shooters, and you do not want this to occur to your covertly armed individual.

To avoid any friendly fire, armed security can wear banners or signs in the event of an emergency that identify them to local law enforcement. The banner could read "Security" or "Police." Whatever method is used to readily distinguish one of your security personnel from the shooter, make certain that responding law enforcement can easily make that distinction. You may want to consider consulting with local police in advance so that they know what to expect. In addition, at least one designated senior manager, who is aware of those covertly armed security personnel, needs to contact 911 when any plainclothes or covertly armed security officers are on the scene of an active shooting and may be engaging with the shooter.

Emergency and/or risk managers should have biannual tabletop and practical exercises in active shooter events. Realistic scenarios should be utilized that truly represent past cases, that use the imagination of the facilitator to mentally challenge those involved, and that go beyond the average exercises. When conducting active shooter practical exercises, you should include local law enforcement in your training. These personnel are great resources, and they can provide advice as well as ensure your safety during the exercise. Exercise plans should include a published scenario where all participants are fully aware of the exercise and its schedule. Never conduct a practical exercise without all potential participants being aware that the event is not real. In May 2010 at a hospital in Las Vegas, Nevada, an emergency preparedness drill was conducted. A police officer, pretending to be a terrorist, stormed into the intensive care unit and produced a handgun, which he pointed at nurses while herding them down a corridor and into a room. Once there, and after several harrowing moments, the officer explained that the whole thing was a training exercise. The staff at that hospital found their exercise more traumatizing than instructive.

Make sure that you have a robust first line of defense. There are some courthouse facilities where law enforcement officers are not deployed as a first line of defense, leaving uniformed and unarmed security officers manning the metal detectors at the front door. There are instead uniformed and armed law enforcement officers who are present, but they are assigned on a random patrol of the facility. This makes the facility vulnerable to attack and is not recommended.

For special events, make sure that you work in conjunction with local law enforcement. Police resources will be extremely valuable in enhancing the safety of the event. Those resources usually include, but are certainly not limited to, bomb sniffing dogs, plainclothes police personnel, and radio access to reinforcements if they are needed. Law enforcement officers and security officials should participate in clearing the event area to ensure that no weapons of any type (firearms or explosive devices) are within the area. Once the area has been cleared, security officials can be strategically placed to retain that secured post. At every special event where the public will gather in large groups, carefully worded signs in all applicable languages should be clearly visible. These signs should advise all those entering the site that they are subject to video surveillance and a search of themselves and their belongings. Exceptions should be made for off-duty and retired law enforcement officers, who should be carrying concealed weapons every time they are in public.

Once the public begins to arrive, there should be specific access areas for them. These funneled choke points force anyone attending the event to enter or exit through restricted areas. Security officers and armed personnel should be posted at all entrances and exits equipped with radios and earphones. Walk-through or handheld metal detectors can also be utilized to increase security. Make sure to screen 100 percent of all incoming individuals. The entry route should be subject to video surveillance, and trained and armed personnel should be stationed along that entry route to observe arriving patrons and notice any potentially suspicious or threatening behavior.

If any of these specialized personnel observe suspicious behavior, they should approach and engage that person. Using tact and diplomacy, they should inquire about the person's reasons for visiting and decide whether they will deny them access. If the sight of metal detectors and trained personnel causes an individual to leave a venue prematurely, that person should be kept under observation and stopped outside the venue. You may want to question them in order to ascertain why they (acting in a suspicious manner) elected to leave the area/venue as opposed to entering.

In the unlikely case that, despite these precautions, an active shooting event does take place, all event personnel (especially uniformed security) need to be well-versed in evacuation techniques, how to shelter and hide, and how to shelter and fight if the need arises. In times of crisis, the public will look to uniformed security to provide direction and guidance to keep them safe. Having a security team that has been thoroughly trained about the threat of an active shooter, has knowledge of event contingency plans, and knows how to implement them is extremely valuable. Tabletop and realistic practical exercises for your security personnel will allow them to gain experience in handling such threats. This prior exposure is invaluable as, if a real threat occurs, your team will have some practical understanding of how to respond. Having the local law enforcement agency participate in the training provides extra credibility and prepares them to work together in the event that a real-life crisis occurs.

Special Events Planners and Organizers

A special event is any type of activity, either indoors or outdoors, in which large numbers of people may gather in a single venue. This includes but not limited to events such as conventions, markets, concerts, athletic competitions, and company gatherings. Any person or organization planning a special event should consult with competent authorities who have a working knowledge of the active shooter threat and know how to address and/or mitigate the event.

Most municipalities have a special events package. This package explains the duties and responsibilities of the event organizer. The application package usually requires that municipal department leaders, such as police and fire departments, sign off on the event. This ensures that the organizers have met certain requirements of safety and have contingency plans in place. In many special events packages, there is no requirement for security or specific mention of the threat of an active shooter. Any entity that fails to adequately address the potential for an active shooter at its event is not fulfilling its civic and moral responsibilities to ensure the safety of its guests and employees.

Take care not to plan your event on a date, or within a date range, where emergency services and resources (police, medical, fire) will be severely limited. For large events, it is vital that emergency services be free to respond immediately. Be aware of other preplanned events that may conflict with yours and therefore stretch emergency resources. Be prepared for authorities to request that your event be moved to a different date.

You should have sufficient police or security present before, during, and after the event that they can hopefully prevent or mitigate any threat. Be aware that not all law enforcement agencies are as proactive as they should be. Ask the supervisor about their level of training and what their contingency plans are if a shooting should occur. Remember that you may be required by that municipality to submit your special event application a minimum of fifteen days to ninety days in advance. This time period should give you enough time to consult with the police about the date and disposition of security at your event.

Take special note that any and all overt/uniformed and armed security officers may be one of the first targets of an active shooter/ assailant prior to unleashing their rampage upon their chosen targets. The shooter/assailant may have surveilled the event and noted the presence of obvious deterrents to their murderous plans and made their adjustments to facilitate their scheme. It is for that reason that the use of more than one armed and covert personnel be deployed at special events. In order to prevent friendly fire, all personnel (overt and covert) that will be armed should meet in private prior to the event for facial/ clothing recognition.

Emergency Medical Services

Emergency medical services will be first responders to an active shooting. It is common for law enforcement to clear an area before medical personnel are allowed in. Although emergency services personnel are compelled to provide care to the critically injured, the survival of the care provider is just as important. A wounded care provider will be unable to provide care for the initial victims of the shooter. Be aware of the potential for a second shooter or an IED.

Consider consulting your local bomb squad about providing training in spotting explosive devises. Protective ballistic vests and helmets should be worn by all emergency medical services personnel responding to an active shooting. Armed law enforcement should also be utilized to guard those who are providing emergency first aid. The protective gear is primarily to protect the medical personnel in the case of an undetected second shooter. It will also protect the emergency responder in the case that the wounded suspect becomes violent while being treated.

Special Needs Facilities

On March 29, 2009, a lone gunman burst into a nursing home in Carthage, North Carolina, and started shooting everyone, barging into the rooms of terrified patients. He ultimately shot and killed seven residents and a nurse who was caring for them. The shooter's estranged wife was a nurse at the facility and was hiding in a bathroom. The shooter wounded three others before being shot by a police officer who confronted the shooter in the hallway.

The patients at a special needs facility may lack the mental or physical capabilities to understand or properly respond to an active shooter. These people are totally dependent on the employees for their personal safety. It is therefore imperative that staff be fully trained in preventing and mitigating the threat of an active shooter. Since escaping from the kill zone will not be possible for a large segment of this clientele, sheltering to hide and sheltering to fight may be the only options. Having at least one competent and armed security officer present and on duty would be highly recommended. Staff members should be taught how to shelter and fight, including learning how to disarm an active shooter. Areas of the facility should be identified where improvised weapons could be found.

The facility should be retrofitted with metal doors on each patient room that open outward into the hallway (to prevent them from being kicked inward) and should be lockable either electronically or with a key (in the possession of the staff). This one change to the doors will provide enhanced protection should you choose to shelter and hide. The facility should be equipped with an audible alarm system. When activating that audible system, the doors should close to each patient's room, locking and securing patients inside their rooms. Staff members should then be required to relinquish the facility to law enforcement personnel, who would open and clear all rooms.

Hospitals

Several past cases illustrate how hospitals are vulnerable to an active shooter. In Baltimore, Maryland, on September 15, 2010, a gunman, reportedly upset about his mother's treatment, opened fire at a hospital. He critically wounded a physician, killed his mother, and then shot himself during a standoff with police. On January 5, 2014, in Daytona Beach, Florida, a man shot himself to death after firing at several cars and attacking a pair of nurses. The suspect crashed his vehicle through the hospital's west gate and fired at several vehicles in the hospital parking lot. No one was injured outside the hospital. He then shot out the glass doors at the entrance to the hospital and then confronted a nurse and patient inside, asking them if they wanted to die that night.

He confronted another patient and nurse in a different room before shooting himself in the head. During the rampage, the suspect also struck two nurses with the butt of the shotgun.

Hospital staff at one local hospital reported that in the event of a "code silver" (an active shooter), each person was supposed to follow the instructions of their supervisor. Health care workers deserve more protection and training instead of relying on their supervisors to lead them through an active shooting. The clientele who visit hospitals will look to hospital workers to assist them. They will assume that each hospital worker has been fully trained on what to do in an emergency. Hospitals typically rely on their local police or facility security to respond and resolve active shootings, but every employee should receive comprehensive training on how to mitigate the threats posed by an active shooter.

The hospital as a whole should ensure that realistic site surveys are conducted, appropriate access control measures are used, and safe rooms are included into the security plan for the hospital. For personal security, all personnel (full-time and casual staff) should be able to choose their preferred techniques and tactics to protect themselves without having to rely on another employee. Considering the number of patients who may be incapable of evacuating, sheltering, or defending themselves, employees may be required to be proactive in their defense in order to safeguard the lives of their patients.

Places of Worship

The church shooting in Charleston, North Carolina, is testament to the need for every place of worship to have a security detail. Such a security team should consist of several members of the congregation who are familiar with the leaders. The team can comprise as few as three people for a small community and at least a dozen for a larger one. A larger team allows team members to have specific responsibilities and the ability to rotate so that members are not on duty at every event. Depending on state law, having several members of that team who are armed, trained, qualified, and prepared mentally to utilize deadly force may be vital. A Security team should include the following positions, each with its own responsibilities: team leader, communications, observers, contact personnel, VIP protection, and armed cover personnel.

A *team leader* will need to be the type of person who has experience in making command decisions and a proven track record. The leader should be armed and part of the decision making process in selecting team members and should participate in their training.

Communications for your team is vital. One person should be designated as the communications leader, who is responsible for logging the time and nature of any incidents, as well as receiving and relaying information to the team as needed. The communications leader is the sole person who should contact emergency services if the need arises. For optimum results, each member should be equipped with a hand-held radio with an earpiece. It is best to choose an individual who performs this sort of task in everyday life. If you don't have such specialized personnel in your community, contact the public safety dispatch supervisor, who may be able to provide training for your designated communications leader.

Observers are placed in strategic locations in and around the church. Positions should include interior and exterior parts of the complex and should cover all entrances, exits, and gathering places. Observers should be trained in how to spot suspicious behaviors and how to observe people who may be carrying concealed firearms. There need to be at least two exterior observers who are present outside the facility while individuals are arriving, while they are leaving, and during the entire event. These observers should be among the last people to leave the church grounds. There should also be at least two interior greeters who are present at least thirty minutes before an event begins. This will reduce the likelihood of a potential threat entering before the greeters are in place. The job of the interior greeters is to be pleasant yet observant. If the greeters were to observe a potential threat, the nature of the threat, along with a physical description, should be immediately communicated to the rest of the security team.

Contact personnel are designated to verbally and/or physically contact a potential threat who has been observed inside the building. These personnel need to know how to approach a potential threat, de-escalate the situation, and if need be, place the person in a restraint hold and escort them from the facility. Each contact person should receive training in defensive tactics for gaining quick physical control over a physically aggressive person. Any person who has to be physically restrained should be arrested for the applicable violation(s) of the law.

VIP protection extends to any person of significance visiting the church, including religious and secular leaders. At least one person should be detailed to this position, and each one should have no more than three VIPs under their protection. The protection team should meet with the VIP prior to the start of the event and explain the particular seating arrangements, the contingency plan, and what movements should be made during an emergency. They should be sufficiently close to the VIP that they can observe and intervene if necessary.

The *armed cover personnel* are the designated shooters in your security team. Other than active duty or retired law enforcement personnel, these people should be the only authorized individuals present who are armed or have access to firearms. They should only use deadly force if a threat exists. If/when such a threat occurs, these individuals should immediately deploy appropriate force to stop the threat. These team members should be extremely familiar with the weapon(s) they may utilize during the event and should regularly qualify on a range to maintain proficiency. The team members should be equipped with the following: at least one handgun, additional ammunition, access to a long gun, such as an AR-15, ballistic vest, neon security banner, flashlight, radio, cell phone, and Bluetooth earpiece. Armed cover personnel should never be placed in a position where they have to physically restrain a problem person, as this will give the individual access to a loaded firearm in the middle of a physical altercation. Therefore, the designated shooter should stay out of all physical altercations.

The building should have at least one safe room. This should be a safe space for VIPs to evacuate to and shelter in while still inside the building. The room should make forced entry by any intruder extremely difficult. The room needs to include communication capabilities for summoning emergency services (police, fire, and ambulances) should the need arise. There should also be items within that area that can be used as weapons should the shooter penetrate the room. The location of the safe room should be shared with local law enforcement. This information is vital when police respond to a location and are attempting to rescue the occupants. In the event of an active shooting, you should only exit the room when your safety has been confirmed by law enforcement. This confirmation can be provided through visual cues or by verifying police presence with the dispatcher.

How your security team should work: With all members of the security team in place, the outside observers should be able to detect any blatant threat as they approach the building. If the subject is capable of concealing their intentions from the outside observers, the subject will be greeted by one of the internal observers upon entering the building. If any of the security team notices a potential threat, the information is immediately relayed to the communications leader, making sure to note the exact threat, the description of the subject, and the location. Depending on the threat type and exact location, the team leader can direct the members to quell the threat and protect the rest of the guests at the same time. If the threat might compromise the safety and security of the church VIPs, they should be escorted to the safe room and sequestered there until the threat is resolved.

If the threat involves deadly force, the members of the wider congregation should be made aware in advance of the identity of the security team members and should be instructed to follow their explicit instructions. With the armed cover personnel and the team leader being the only armed individuals on your team, they are the logical choices to engage the suspect. The communications leader should immediately contact local law enforcement dispatch, advising them of the current situation and that members of their security team are armed. It is imperative the physical description of the armed cover team members be communicated to the police dispatcher. As soon as possible, all armed security team members should deploy their neon security banners to avoid potential friendly fire from responding law enforcement. If the armed subject has been neutralized, the communications leader should be advised and should advise the police dispatcher. All armed members of the team should immediately holster their weapons and prepare for the arrival of law enforcement. In the event that law enforcement arrives on scene prior to the threat being neutralized, armed security personnel should relinquish command of the scene as soon as possible to the responding law enforcement personnel. Unless the law enforcement personnel make a specific demand for the armed security members to continue engaging the subject, security members should disengage and allow law enforcement to take over the scene and either neutralize the subject or take them into custody.

In the event of activities taking place outside the usual facilities, your security team should gather security intelligence in advance. The team leader should conduct a site survey to determine potential risks, vulnerabilities, and areas to use for sheltering should the need arise.

An example of how a security team can work is evident from the church shooting in Colorado Springs, Colorado, on December 7, 2007. A gunman opened fire at 12:30 a.m., killing two people at the Youth with a Mission Center in Denver. Witnesses said the man asked to spend the night there and opened fire with a handgun when he was turned down. They described him as a young man, perhaps twenty, in a dark jacket and cap. The following day, at New Life Church in Colorado Springs, a gunman wearing a trench coat and carrying a high-powered rifle opened fire in the parking lot and later walked into the church as services concluded, killing two people. About 7,000 people were in and around the church at the time of the shooting. Church security had fifteen to twenty volunteer security officers inside at the time of the attack. The number had been beefed up after the shootings the night before in Arvada. A female church member, who volunteers as a security guard, shot the armed assailant, who was found with a rifle and two handguns and may have had as many as a thousand rounds of ammunition. The security officer said that she saw the shooter coming through the doors, took cover, and waited for him to get closer before identifying herself and taking down the shooter. The female security officer was one of about a dozen volunteer security guards at the church, half of whom are armed. The guards were licensed, trained, and screened, and were church members. It was estimated that forty rounds had been fired inside the church, leaving what looked like a war scene. The pastor credited the security officer with preventing more bloodshed. It appears that the suspect had been kicked out of the program three years prior and, during the past few weeks, had sent different forms of hate mail to the program and its director.

Part 6

Trends in the Behaviors of Active Shooters

The best predictor of future behavior is past behavior. From events that continue to occur, the active shooter does not appear to going away. In fact, the level of violence and sophistication of the assailants only seems to increase. Below, I explain some trends that are visible in past shootings, in the hope that this will provide some insight into potential future attacks and allow the development of defensive strategies. Being aware of how these events are linked allows others to see how and where the assailants may choose to inflict future harm. Consider that future assailants will likely incorporate two or more of these elements in their particular attacks.

Killing others in their home prior to the attack: In many cases, the shooters started their killing sprees by killing others in or around their residences before going to a secondary location. Prior cases include Austin, Texas; Blacksburg, Virginia (Virginia Tech); Newtown, Connecticut; and Santa Barbara, California.

Extensive planning: Premeditated assailants will go through several mental and physical phases prior to committing their crimes. During this time, the future killer will prepare for the event, conduct research, and plan in great detail for the deadly event. In past cases, the suspect took a significant period of time to collect weapons and ammunition. The suspects even considered the victims' locations and reactions as they stalked and murdered them. Prior cases include Littleton, Colorado (Columbine); Blacksburg, Virginia (Virginia Tech); Oslo, Norway; Santa Barbara, California; San Bernardino, California; Cumming, Georgia; and Istanbul, Turkey.

Internet research into past shooters: Several of the shooters had performed research into past active shooters. Whether the shooter intended to surpass the researched killers or to learn from those tactics is unknown. Past cases include Newtown, Connecticut; Columbia, Maryland; Sparks, Nevada; Santa Barbara, California; and Orlando, Florida.

Multiple crime scene locations: In several cases, the active shooter has committed murders in other locations prior to entering the location where the shooting spree began. Past cases include Blacksburg, Virginia (Virginia Tech); Newtown, Connecticut; Fort Hood, Texas; Santa Barbara, California; Las Vegas, Nevada; Chattanooga, Tennessee; and Istanbul, Turkey.

Multiple weapons: In many cases, the suspects used a combination of weapons in each of the events. These include several handguns, at least one long gun, knives, IEDs, and even vehicles. Past cases include Austin, Texas (tower sniper); Blacksburg, Virginia (Virginia Tech); Cedarville, California; Aurora, Colorado; Santa Barbara, California; San Bernardino, California; Cumming, Georgia; Fort Hood, Texas; London, England; Las Vegas, Nevada; Chattanooga, Tennessee; and Orlando, Florida.

Use of improvised explosive devices: Cases where the suspect deployed home-made or other explosives include Littleton, Colorado; Aurora, Colorado; San Bernardino, California; Cumming, Georgia; and Istanbul, Turkey.

Shooter(s) wearing body armor: There are several cases where active shooters have arrived at the scene of their crimes wearing body armor. Those cases include North Hollywood, California; Aurora, Colorado; San Bernardino, California; and Cumming, Georgia.

Use of social media, manifestos, and other communications: Several of the killers utilized social media, posted their ramblings online, or otherwise chronicled their crimes prior to their events occurring. These cases include Blacksburg, Virginia (Virginia Tech); Oslo, Norway; Newtown, Connecticut; Columbia, Maryland; Santa Barbara, California; Las Vegas, Nevada; Charleston, South Carolina; and Orlando, Florida.

Known mental health issues: Shooters sometimes have significant and/or acute mental health problems. These include Austin, Texas; Blacksburg, Virginia (Virginia Tech); Aurora, Colorado; Carson City, Nevada; Newtown, Connecticut; Fort Hood, Texas; Santa Barbara, California; Seattle, Washington; Chattanooga, Tennessee; and Ft. Lauderdale, Florida International Airport.

Multiple assailants: Although there are currently only a few cases where multiple suspects are involved, there is always a distinct possibility that more than one shooter is involved. Past cases include Littleton, Colorado; Las Vegas, Nevada; Mumbai, India; Nairobi, Kenya; London, England; Jerusalem, Israel; Paris, France; San Bernardino, California; Temple of Hatshepsut, Egypt; and Istanbul, Turkey.

Victims specific to gender: Some of the active shooters have stated that they specifically target women because of some special hatred. Past cases include Luby's Cafeteria, Kileen, Texas, and Santa Barbara, California.

Female shooters: Women have also committed mass shootings, either alone or as part of a team. Cases include Goletta, California; Cedarville, California; Las Vegas, Nevada; and San Bernardino, California.

Citizen Intervention

Rather than to leave citizens to their own devices when they need help the most, this work is designed to provide average citizens with the tools, tactics, and techniques they need to best defend themselves.

Citizens have demonstrated that they cannot wait for the arrival of law enforcement to stop violent aggression and that they can act independently and successfully to fight for their own safety and the safety of others. These examples are prime illustrations of appropriate actions and citizen intervention that helped prevent additional carnage from occurring. It is apparent that these intervening citizens felt they could not just hide and hope, and that they needed to take on the assailants. These cases prove that citizen intervention can be done without tactical errors to stop the murderous rampage of an active shooter.

On January 8, 2011, in a Safeway parking lot in Arizona, US Representative Giffords and eighteen others were shot during a constituent meeting. Six people died. The suspect used a semi-automatic pistol, and during his reloading, he dropped the magazine to the firearm. One citizen picked up the loaded magazine. Another citizen struck the shooter in the back of the head with a folding chair, while a third citizen tackled the shooter. Although one of the citizens who assisted in subduing the shooter was legally armed, the citizen arrived after the shooting had stopped and did not have to draw his weapon.

On February 27, 2012, at a high school in Chardon, Ohio, three male students died and two other students were hospitalized after a shooting occurred inside the school's cafeteria. The shooter was a student with .22 caliber handgun, who was chased from the school by a male teacher. The suspect was arrested outside shortly afterward by law enforcement.

On April 9, 2014, a mass stabbing and slashing knife attack took place at a high school in Murrysville, Pennsylvania, where twenty-five people were injured. The suspect, a sixteen-year-old male student, was armed with two knives and was wearing all black clothing. The attack occurred in the school's crowded hallways just prior to the start of the school day. The suspect was described (by the victims) as emotionless. When tackled by a school official and a fellow student, the suspect reportedly said that his work was not done yet. The school's resource officer was wounded during the attack and did not participate in the final apprehension of the suspect.

On June 5, 2014, a lone gunman armed with a shotgun opened fire at a Christian university in Seattle, Washington. The shooting killed one person and injured three others before a student building monitor using pepper spray was able to disarm the gunman as he tried to reload his weapon. Several other students jumped on top of the shooter, pinning him down until police arrived. The shooter had additional rounds of ammunition and a knife.

On August 21, 2015, a man boarded a high-speed train from Amsterdam to Paris. The man was armed with an assault rifle, a handgun, and a knife. There were several Americans on board the train, and upon hearing the gunman loading one of his weapons inside the train's restroom, they decided to take action. The three worked to overpower the gunman, but he was able to fire at least one shot and injure one man. The gunman was physically subdued, restrained, and held for authorities, who boarded the train at their next stop.

Although some organizations may be capable of having armed intervention, private security officers, resource officers, or even police officers present at their facilities, they alone cannot always stop or deter an armed assailant. Legally armed citizens should not be prohibited from carrying their concealed weapons on them into most of these places. During the summer and fall of 2015, the police chief of Detroit, Michigan, advised that citizens within his city obtain concealed license permits. The chief (and others) believe that legally arming its law-abiding citizens would cause a reduction in violent crimes against them. Organizations should take these numerous shootings and vicious attacks to heart and remove all obstacles that currently stop people from accessing the information they need to protect themselves. Potential victims of any active shooter deserve to know what to do during a killing rampage long before the event occurs and therefore not to have to make up their tactics in the heat of the moment.

Law Enforcement Agency Facilitation

There are several things that law enforcement can do to assist or facilitate the average citizen's defense against an active shooter. They can provide realistic training when they are providing instruction to citizen groups. Instead of advocating that citizens simply hide and hope that law enforcement will respond in time, police should provide concerned citizens with the same training that these officers would use if they were in a similar situation and unarmed. As an example, what tactics would three or four officers who were off-duty and unarmed use against an active shooter? I doubt that they would choose to hide under a table or in a closet, hoping that armed law enforcement found them before the shooter. They would instead team up with others willing to fight for their lives and be prepared to defend themselves if necessary. The average citizens deserve the same training so they can use the same tactics.

Several years ago, legislation was passed that allowed all retired law enforcement officers in good standing to obtain a concealed weapons permit that is valid in all states. Part of the rationale was the recognition that having an extra trained and armed individual at the scene of a violent crime would increase the chances of innocent people surviving the encounter. Law enforcement agencies can add to this concept by including retired officers in their active shooter training classes. This provides the retired officer with up-to-date training on the subject as well as familiarization and face-to-face recognition with local law enforcement personnel. The retired law enforcement officer would also be able to obtain a banner that could be deployed during an active shooting. This banner is used to provide immediate recognition of a plainclothes law enforcement officer and reduce the likelihood of a being hit by friendly fire. All retired law enforcement officers should be authorized by law and encouraged by school district officials to carry their weapons on campus. These retired officers have demonstrated that they are responsible individuals and are unlikely to leave a gun in a drawer or bathroom stall. These officers are also sufficiently educated about when and how to engage a suspect who would pose a deadly threat to the public. Colleges and universities should also authorize retired police officers to carry their concealed weapons on campus. These retired officers would be in plain clothes and could supplement the law enforcement effort on each campus. These officers could be enticed and rewarded by perks such as free entry into college events and classes. If an active shooting were to occur with this supplemental force present, the assailant could be met by one of these armed and trained retired officers, who could either neutralize the threat or suppress the deadly activity until the arrival of on-duty and uniformed law enforcement.

All police dispatch and emergency communications could create individual and unique radio call signs for all personnel whether on duty, off duty, or retired. In the event that an officer (especially off duty or retired) needs to communicate with police dispatch (via telephone or a police radio), these officers could utilize their call signs, which would instantly alert the dispatcher as to who they are. The dispatcher could then alert responding on-duty officers as to the identity of the off-duty officer. This identity facilitates the safety of the off-duty officer and dramatically reduces the potential for friendly fire.

And lastly, each law enforcement jurisdiction can develop, teach, and implement a citywide audible alert system any time an active shooter/assailant crime is in progress. This audible alert, coupled with a brief cellular text message, would be activated in the same manner as the amber alert system notifying everyone living within that particular jurisdiction. This notification system can be sent to cellular telephones, bill boards, electronic highway notification signs, and electronic media to include television and radio stations, all designed to alert the citizens within an affected area. This notification would also alert citizens to prevent them from accidental entry into or passage through such dangerous areas.

Conclusion

What have we learned about the active shooter? It appears this threat is seemingly never-ending. There are some factors inside and outside of our control. We are not able to predict the exact identity and method of the shooter. Past shooting events include males and females, children and adults, and various ethnicities. They occur inside and outside the United States and in both public and private places within our society. There has been no sure-fire way to detect who the next active shooter might be. Active shootings are usually premeditated, and the shooters have planned the exact day and time for the attack. They will have brought with them all the weapons they desire to carry out the murderous rampage.

Shooters have consistently demonstrated they will approach and enter the premises with their weapons concealed on their person, inside some type of bag, or in full view. Although we can make it more difficult for an active shooter to gain access to a location or to access weapons, there is almost nothing that can be done to completely prevent an active shooter who is determined to kill people. Some assailants have even resorted to the use of edged weapons, while others began their killing with a firearm and, when they ran out of ammunition, resorted to knives.

We know the shooter is motivated by a number of factors. As long as there are sick and twisted individuals bent on killing people within our society, these types of cases may never stop, and the list of locations, the identities of the shooters, and their rationale for killing will increase seemingly unabated with unpredictability.

What we are able to do is use our situational awareness and observation skills to be aware of the people around us, especially those approaching our location. With the right knowledge, we should be able to determine if someone is a potential threat within a few seconds. There are things you can do in your ordinary life if you notice suspicious activity or the presence of firearms in unusual places. Any person or persons holding a firearm in their hands (handgun or long gun) or inside a case is definitely a threat to everyone's safety.

One day, I was exiting my car in the parking lot of a martial arts school where I was about to teach a class on active shooter defense. As I walked through the parking lot carrying a large backpack and a shotgun carrying case, I received several curious looks from drivers within the parking lot. Those drivers failed to take any further action beyond some curious looks. They should have immediately left the area and called police to report the suspicious circumstances. In these times, it is better to assume wrongful intentions whenever a firearm is observed in an unusual setting. As a law abiding citizen, I have no reservations about being contacted by law enforcement and explaining my actions. This is better than allowing people to walk freely through an area carrying firearms. Noticing a person who may pose a potential threat to the safety of innocent people provides an opportunity for individuals or law enforcement to take actions that might reduce the threat. Those actions can range from the evacuation of the immediate area to maintaining a closer observation until the person has demonstrated and confirmed that they are not a threat.

Parents, siblings, family members, and close friends who notice alarming or threatening behaviors need to immediately intervene, interrupting a potential course of conduct that could lead to deadly consequences. On August 18, 2014, police in Pasadena, California, arrested two teenage boys who were plotting to kill three high school employees and at least two fellow students, all named targets who worked at or attended South Pasadena High School. Once the police received information posted on social media, they kept the teens under constant surveillance. The teens were attempting to obtain weapons, such as submachine guns, rifles, bombs, and propane for explosives. The teens were also researching how to assemble and fire the weapons. This arrest is a prime example of the use of public threat management principles and then acting on threat information to stop a shooting from occurring.

A number of active shooters have documented acute mental health issues. Currently, there are no systems in place to prevent any person with related mental health issues from obtaining, owning, accessing, or possessing one or more firearms. A prospective shooter who is seeking to obtain a firearm just needs to maintain composure during the traditional gun-store purchasing process, and there are no comprehensive background or mental health checks. At the present date, the name of a person wants to purchase a firearm must be submitted to a database inquiry to determine criminal history. There is no such database for the acutely mentally ill or mentally impaired, as this would violate the privacy of the mentally ill person. Past shooters have purchased and amassed firearms and ammunition from reputable gun dealers prior to their deadly events. Until those issues are properly sorted out and appropriate legislation can be passed by lawmakers and consistently enforced, the seriously mentally ill or impaired individual will have access to firearms.

Legislation also needs to encompass other individuals who may aid, knowingly or unknowingly, a mentally ill individual in gaining access to a firearm. In June 2014, California legislators considered passing a law where concerned loved ones will have the ability to obtain a legal restraining order when a person's mental health appears to be at risk. The police may then seize the weapons temporarily and put that person on a blacklist. This law is reportedly currently in effect in Texas, Indiana, and Connecticut. There is no set of laws, however, that can stop the active shooter from obtaining one or more deadly weapons.

The places where firearms are absolutely and strictly prohibited are places where screening of people and their property is located at the entrances to the facility. In those places, there are usually armed personnel to support the legal prohibition of firearms and to protect them from armed attack. If a facility is not prepared to competently and successfully engage in the armed defense of the citizens within the premises, they should not advocate nor mandate disarming the legally armed individuals. In that case, legally armed individuals should be allowed to carry their concealed weapons within to allow them to defend themselves. Along with this authorization, the legally armed defender needs to be taught how to successfully engage the active shooter, thus eliminating the threat and decreasing the shooter's casualty rate, as well as ensuring the safety of everyone within that area.

The only thing that will definitely stop an armed assailant from murdering innocent people is armed and trained intervention by people who are capable of using deadly force. In short, we should authorize legally armed and trained individuals to carry their concealed weapons into the very same places where these active shooters have been engaging and killing defenseless citizens. If guns are taken from the hands of all law-abiding defenders, criminals and mentally ill persons will still be able to access firearms and use them against those now-defenseless citizens. If, for some reason, all the guns were removed from society, killers would still find other deadly weapons to use against the unarmed citizenry. One youthful assailant from Murrysville, Pennsylvania, demonstrated that he could inflict carnage and pandemonium by using two edged weapons. If, for some reason, knives were outlawed, the assailants of tomorrow would find yet another innovative way to inflict their personal revenge.

The American public deserves more than lip service and being told to wait for authorities to come to our rescue, even though that response can come too late. How many rounds could be fired during those minutes while the police are responding? How many lives could be lost during the time it takes for police to be notified, respond, locate the threat, and adequately address it? If more individuals were authorized to carry concealed firearms and educated in their use, there would be no need to rely on someone else to come and save us.

Every entity has a moral and civic responsibility to do the best it can to protect the lives of all who enter their property. Organizations need to recognize that threats emanate from within their ranks as well as from outside. We cannot rely on contemporary organizational supervisors who are unwilling and/or unable to notice and act upon the pre-incident suspicious behavior. Once that behavior is noticed, the organization needs to take action. Unfortunately, there is no exact profile of behaviors that will absolutely guarantee that a person is, or will become, the next active shooter. The best that can be done is to cite behaviors noted in an organizational setting that signal that a particular person needs immediate intervention. At our worksites and in our private lives, we can employ the use of threat management principles to aid our organization or family in thwarting potential shooters.

We can also educate our unarmed citizen population by providing them with the best logical information about how to respond to an active shooting. Citizens should no longer have to resort to the "hide and hope" strategy. Citizens can be taught realistic techniques and tactics that can save their lives until the arrival of law enforcement. Defenders can be educated and trained, and they practice practical, easy, and effective techniques to use against their assailant.

From the perspective of a former law enforcement officer, we cannot deploy police on every corner, in every restaurant, or inside every classroom. Nor can we depend on politicians to really commit and follow through with appropriate legislation. We also cannot depend on organizations and our employers to supply us with the best or even sufficient training to effectively observe and mitigate the shooter. It has been my experience that most of these leaders will appoint someone to construct a paperwork solution to a very complex problem, just to say they have given thought to and addressed the threat. Now is the time for a paradigm shift. We need to stop waiting for someone else to come to our rescue and save us in the nick of time when we are capable of effectively taking care of ourselves, at least until the proper authorities do arrive.

In the school shooting from Chardon, Ohio, on February 27, 2012, the entire event took forty-seven seconds from the time the first shot was fired (killing three students) to when the suspect fled the building being chased by a teacher/coach. Perhaps the shooter (a high school student) would have stayed longer and killed more people if he had not been challenged by an unarmed male teacher who chased him out of the school. Although I do not agree with the tactics and how the challenge took place, it did, however, stop the killing.

We have to move away from ineffective and inefficient training that does little to actually save lives. Most trainers simply tell their students to run and hide. Even when fighting suggested as an option, the instructors are frequently unable to offer specific and detailed instruction in how best to actually fight for one's life. Organizational politics consistently gets in the way of any attempt to offer new or improved training solutions. If organizations continue in this vein and continue to not allow realistic training, they should not be surprised when they are personally held liable in civil proceedings for negligence.

We no longer have the luxury to wait and see what will happen, as it is clear that the standard training is not working. This complacent attitude has cost countless lives and will likely cost many more in the future. Men, women, and children who have been the victims of these shootings deserve justice. The failure of the authorities to adequately address all the complexities surrounding this threat is an insult to the memory of all the victims of active shooters.

On June 7, 2013, in Santa Monica, California, a lone gunman started with a domestic dispute and a fire at a home, followed by a series of shootings near and on the campus of Santa Monica College. Six people were killed, including the suspect, and four people were injured in the incident. The gunman, a twenty-three-year-old, was killed by police officers when he exchanged gunfire with them at the

Santa Monica College library. Authorities investigated up to nine crime scenes believed to be tied to the thirteen-minute-long shooting spree. Imagine what could have happened if a citizen involved in that melee had been educated about a personal survival plan and armed.

It is evident that people bent on shooting, stabbing, and killing people are not concerned with rules and regulations, while the rest of us must be constricted by these same rules that allow the murderers to roam free among us. While experts debate the rationale and attempt to ascertain the motives and sanity of the shooter, these shootings have and will continue unabated at a different time and place, with different victims.

Imagine a place where an active shooter produces a firearm and begins a murderous campaign, only to be met immediately by someone already present at that location who is educated, empowered, and prepared to address the active shooter. That brave defender either disarms the shooter of the weapon or utilizes their legally possessed and concealed firearm to successfully engage the active shooter, using deadly force to counter deadly force.

As of July 1, 2014, the state of Georgia has a new law regarding guns, allowing residents to carry firearms into bars, nightclubs, classrooms, and government buildings in a measure slammed by anti-weapon activists as a "dangerous kill bill." The law, which critics are calling the "guns everywhere law," is considered one of the most extreme pro-gun bills in the country. Under its provisions, residents with proper gun permits will be allowed to carry guns at a number of previously off-limits places. The carry laws do not allow people to carry their weapons into secure areas of the Airport. With shootings in areas of worship, religious leaders will be allowed to let people take guns into churches. Georgia's governor, Nathan Deal, signed the Safe Carry Protection Act after the state's Republican-controlled General Assembly overwhelmingly passed the measure on the last day of the legislative session. The law reduces the penalty against a permit holder caught with a gun on a college campus to a fine instead of a misdemeanor. Any licensed gun owner from Georgia and visitors from twenty-eight other states may carry guns into bars, as long as they do not consume alcohol, and into government offices that don't have metal detectors or security guards screening visitors. School districts may appoint staff members to carry a weapon. Similar legislation has popped up in other states, including Missouri, Oklahoma, and Tennessee, but the Georgia law has garnered so much attention because it expands carrying rights in multiple areas with a single law.

On July 25, 2014, a forty-nine-year-old man walked into the psychiatric unit in Darby, Pennsylvania, with his caseworker. The two went into a psychiatrist's office, where an argument erupted. Staff members heard loud arguing inside the doctor's office and opened the door, only to notice the man had a gun pointed at the doctor. The staff quietly closed the door and called 911. Gunshots were heard a short time later, and the patient shot the caseworker. The doctor was able to take cover, obtain his firearm, and engage the shooter. A struggle ensued that spilled out into the hallway. Another doctor and caseworker jumped in to help secure the patient's firearm. The hospital has a policy banning anyone except on-duty law enforcement officers from carrying weapons on its campus. The Yeadon police chief said that he believed the doctor had saved lives. Without that firearm, the patient could have gone out into the hallway and just walked down the offices until he ran out of ammunition.

The exchange of gunfire occurred on the third floor of a Wellness Center, a 204-bed community teaching hospital. There are no surveillance cameras in the doctor's office or the waiting area outside, as well as no metal detectors. After the shooting, patients waiting in the lobby on the first floor (most of them were elderly people with walkers and canes) reported a tense scene when police arrived and ordered everyone out.

On October 24, 2014, a shooting occurred at a high school in Marysville, Washington. The shooter, a popular fourteen-year-old student invited (via text) several of his friends and family members (all fellow students) to lunch in the school's cafeteria. The shooter met his invited guests in the cafeteria, produced a .40 caliber semi-automatic handgun and, without any provocation or warning, methodically shot his invited guests, including two of his own cousins, killing at least four other students. After the shooter critically wounded these students, he died from a self-inflicted gunshot wound to the head. This school was one of three schools given a $10 million federal grant to improve mental health services, partly to address the active shooter threat. No matter what else is done to prevent an event from occurring, and despite the fact that armed police can and do respond within minutes, the most important element is how the participants, no matter their age, respond to the incident to save their own lives.

The plethora of attacks and shootings throughout the United States and internationally underscores how private citizens at all levels deserve to be authorized and empowered to care for their own safety and the safety of others. In February 2015, the terrorist group Al-Shabaab produced a video in which they called for attacks on shopping malls within the United States and Canada. The group celebrated the 2013 terrorist attack at the Westgate shopping mall in Nairobi, Kenya, where more than sixty people were killed. In April 2015, this same terrorist group claimed responsibility for the attack on a college campus in Kenya where 147 victims were shot and killed. The killers separated Muslims from Christians, requiring some people who claimed to be Muslims to recite a Muslim prayer. All four of the armed gunmen were subsequently killed in a gun battle with security forces. At least two survivors told their stories. One survivor smeared blood from other victims on herself and mixed in with the casualties. Another victim secreted herself inside a cabinet and did not come out for over twenty hours, well after the armed siege had concluded. And lastly, from the gunman at the Ft. Lauderdale, Florida airport who savagely shot eleven people in the baggage claim area killing five of them. There appears to be a link that indicates shooter/assailants are not deterred from their murderous attacks and seem to exploit the weaknesses of any security system.

We are well into an era where others who are sworn to protect us cannot be there in the most critical moments, nor can they foresee all the possibilities, locations and methods the next shooter/assailant will use. Lives are lost by the second. It is when ordinary people with the right training are given the *authority and permission* to use all of their senses to protect themselves and others that the massacre of innocent lives will subside.

My hope is that this book provides a different paradigm for any and all potential victims of an active shooter and for policymakers and administrators in all types of organizations who feel that something more can be done. I sincerely hope that the content is empowering and allows the reader to become thoroughly knowledgeable of the deadly threat the active shooter/assailant has posed and will continue to pose. I would like for leaders to embrace a different paradigm and no longer be paralyzed by fear of change. They should allow people within their areas of influence the flexibility to match the deadly threat posed by the active shooter with appropriate force and not tie their hands by unreasonable policies that provide a significant advantage to the shooter and place any defender at a huge disadvantage.

Acknowledgements

....

I would like to thank all of the people that assisted to make this work possible. The initial praise goes to God, who has been my Lord and Savior, for I know firsthand that he has dispatched guardian angels to guide me through numerous dangerous environments and situations throughout my life. I need to thank all of my martial arts instructors (Stanford McNeal, Alexander Archie, Donnie Williams, and Steve (Sanders) Muhammad), who provided me with the knowledge base to craft the expeditious techniques by which assailants can be disarmed and incapacitated. I would also like to thank the many dedicated martial artists at 360 Martial Arts, especially their founder, Master Paul Reyes, for allowing his students (Boris Tavcar, my long-time friend, and his son Jacob) to help with the knife and firearm disarming movements, and Terri Svetich, who photographed these personal defensive techniques. I would also thank Jeffrey Bonano and Derek Kroshus for all of their tireless work in photography and video filming and editing for this work, as well as the person who completed the initial editing for this work, Sheira Cohen.

I would also like to acknowledge my family who has continued to inspire, love and support me through all my literary work and the self- defense of others. I love each and every one of you! Lastly, I need to acknowledge all those who have been victims of an Active Shooter/ Assailant and pray for their souls to rest in God's grace and grant their surviving family peace. It is through their sacrifices, their pain and their tragic loss of life that truly inspired me to impart these strategies and techniques. My single purpose for this work is to assist in saving the lives of others who may someday be in grave danger from such violent offenders.

About the Author

....

Joseph B. Walker is the owner of Leading Edge Threat Mitigation, which provides real-world tactical and technical information on how to mitigate any number of threats. Their course topics range from active shooter mitigation and protection against stalkers to self-defense courses for civilian and law enforcement personnel. Joseph utilizes his expertise as a ninth-degree black belt in martial arts with two world karate championship titles to formulate techniques that are practical, easy, and effective against any assailant. Joseph is also the author of *Self-Defense Tactics and Techniques.* He has appeared on numerous local radio and television programs covering threat mitigation strategies for stalking, workplace violence, and shootings.

During Joseph's twenty-five-year law enforcement career with the Reno Police Department and as a member of the Reno Police honor guard, he performed several engagements as a professional trumpet player at the National Law Enforcement Peace Officer's Memorial in Washington, DC. Joseph was certified as a physical fitness instructor by the FBI and provided martial arts instruction to the Washoe County Sheriff's Department and Reno Police Department defensive tactics instructors, as well as a host of local, state, and federal law enforcement agencies. Walker has performed dignitary protection and threat assessments for President Gerald Ford, Bernice King, Martin Luther King III, Merle-Evers Williams, and Hank Aaron. Joseph authored the *Police Officer's Guide to Stalking* handbook for the Reno Police Department.

Upon retiring from the Reno Police Department, Joseph worked for the United States Department of Homeland Security, where he provided training for several state and federal agencies on active shooter defense and the threat of shoulder-fired missiles against commercial aircraft. Joseph attended training on behavior detection provided by Homeland Security and on small-unit tactics and dignitary protection provided by the United States Secret Service.

Due to his extensive background in the martial arts, threat mitigation, law enforcement defensive tactics, and use-of-force options, he is sought out for criminal and civil trials and case preparations as an expert witness.

Printed in the United States
By Bookmasters